FINDING 40

ALISHA RAMASAR

ALISHA RAMASAR

· · · · · · · · · · · · · · · · · ·

FINDING FORTY

Availa Publishing Group

About the Author

Alisha Ramasar is a delightful cocktail of sunshine and sass with a dash of strategic genius. An award-winning International Cannes Lion recipient, she's the mastermind behind Smooch Skincare and the author of "Picture Perf*cked" - a book inspired by her two princess-superhero daughters, who remind her daily that she's a mom first and Wonder Woman second. Alisha doesn't just think outside the box - she remodels it, paints it in bright colours, and turns it into something that makes you wonder why you ever bothered with boring old boxes in the first place. Despite her best intentions to kick back and relax, Alisha has a habit of saying "yes" to more sh*t that keeps her busier than ever. One day, she'll learn to say "no." Today is not that day.

This book is the brainchild of an anxious late-thirty-something mom who has mastered the art of turning chaos into a giggle. Every name, character, place, and event is a playful exaggeration of reality, spun from a mind running on caffeine and daydreams. Inspired by the wild ride that is everyday life, these stories are meant to be taken with a grain of salt - and maybe a glass of wine. Consider it your friendly reminder that turning 40 doesn't make you old - it just makes you better at faking it.

For my Daughters, Ava Saria & Aila Sena. One day, my loves, this book will hopefully help you understand part of the journey of being a woman. Albeit, times will likely be very different when you are my age. I believe there will always be a space in a woman's life for the gentle reminder that this is life and it's going to be ok. Be kind and have courage, my babies!

Mommy loves you more than you will ever know.

Possible.

To my Amazing Husband,
My life, my love - thank you for being mine and for loving me the way you do. You are my everything.
I love you…. more!

Dear Readers,

When I embarked on writing this manuscript, I thought it would be a collection of some of my big and beautiful thoughts about turning 40. Little did I know, or what kind of hit me sideways - was that writing this manuscript would be a therapy for understanding the fundamental shifts in life.

Sure, that sounds a little heavy for someone who has just headed around the sun 38 times. But for what it's worth, the journey to forty is a journey worth writing about. A journey worth acknowledging. A journey of self-realisation. A journey to the infamous "I don't give a toot about other people's perceptions of me." Hopefully, you will stop trying so hard to please others. You take control and focus on what's important.

So, with these lofty expectations hanging over my impending 40th birthday like a glittering piñata, I hope these anecdotes and pearls of wisdom resonate with you. Here's to let you know:

- You're not alone in this crazy ride.

- It's perfectly fine not to have it all figured out.

- It's all part of the grand adventure.

- And apparently, 40 is just 30 with better wine.

So buckle up, enjoy the read, and feel free to slide into my DMs on Instagram @byalisharamasar—I'd love to hear your thoughts and stories or just share a virtual glass of wine!

With all the love, laughter, and a healthy dose of "I'm too old for this sh*t,"

Alisha

Chapter One

Act II.

No Script. Just Improv.

There comes a point in life when, generally, we can't help but wonder what's next. Will I age like fine wine or like a bottle of cheap rosé left in the sun? Will I finally stop pretending I don't give a damn about what Karen thinks, or will I just get better at hiding it?

As I occasionally ponder on these thoughts, I reflect on the famous words once said by the great philosopher Natasha Beddingfield, 'the rest is still unwritten.' Frankly, this sounds a lot like the universe telling me to wing it. So, here we go.

A few years after my first book, Picture Perf*cked, I am, admittedly, a little older, thankfully wiser, and, God, I hope, roughly around the same weight. Still no self-proclaimed expert in the art of womanhood - but I've found a passion in writing, have a decent amount of first-hand experiences, and a weird joy in releasing all inhibitions on paper.

If you found yourself here at this very point - it's probably a sign that it's time to take a break, relax, and find peace in knowing that your crazy is my crazy, too.

Contemplating writing again wasn't such a quick and easy decision. Whilst I love the freedom it gives me, I wanted to make sure that if I were going to attempt to head down this road again, it would form part of my own growth, my own journey, and therefore, I can continue to be authentic and relevant for that stage in my life.
Hopefully, with these nuggets of personal and inspired life experiences, you too can find peace in knowing it's ok, not to be ok. And most importantly - you are not alone.
I had the title of this book set with a particular journey in mind.
All I had to do was wait for the motivation and little voices in my head to start speaking to me.

And speak unto thou they did indeed. Usually, at the most inconvenient times, too, like when I'm in the shower or trying to sneak in a quiet moment of my time. But here's the thing about those little voices: they actually don't care about your schedule. They show up, they demand to be heard, and more often than not, they have their timing aligned to just when you think you've got things figured out. It's as if the universe is playing a little trick on you and awaiting applause like a perfectly timed moment on the sitcom Friends - "The one where life laughs at you for thinking your work is done."

So here I am, once again surrendering to those persistent nudges, opening the floodgates to a new set of stories, epiphanies, and revelations. If I've learned anything over the past few years, it's that growth doesn't stop when you hit a milestone, publish a book, or survive a global pandemic while raising tiny humans. Growth is this relentless force that drags you forward, whether you're ready or not. It shows up in the little moments - like if you're deciding between another slice of cheesecake or whether you should head to bed at a reasonable hour. Or even if you're balancing the wild ride of motherhood with the equally wild expectations of womanhood.

It sneaks up in those beautifully chaotic moments of life, where everything's a hot mess when you're tripping over your own feet and when you start wondering, "What the hell am I even doing?" That's where the real magic happens, amid the stumbles, fumbles, and facepalms. We rediscover ourselves again and again, rewiring our brains to ditch perfection and start embracing the wonderfully messy realness.

And honestly? That's exactly what we should be aiming for!

If there's one thing I hope you take away from this book, it's that realness is, in my opinion, the secret ingredient in life. One that is often hard to find. However, when you do find it, it will be in the moments where you happen to let your guard down, when you laugh at your own ridiculousness, and when you let others experience and see the real you. Those are the moments that matter. So, here I am before you, claiming that if we're going to navigate this next chapter of life together, I say we do it with a healthy dose of humour, a side of self-compassion, and maybe a chilled glass of wine (let's avoid that sun-warmed rosé, shall we?). So let's raise a metaphorical glass (or a literal one - no judgement here!) and toast to winging it, to knowing that the rest is indeed still unwritten, and to embracing the unknown with open arms and a sense of adventure.

As any good story should begin...

Once upon a time.

Sitting at the country club whilst my daughters and husband are playing golf, probably to the outside world, looking like I'm pretty put together sipping on my cappa. A lady walks up to my table with a tub of fruit in her hand. She seems uncertain in her approach, and to be honest, I'm also a little uncertain at this stage. Did I take her seat? Am I blocking her view? Did we know each other? Am I supposed to know her? The questions come into my mind steadily and fast.

She bends over and calls for her one-year-old kid to come out from under my table. "Apologies, he's been chasing this pigeon; sorry to disturb you and your cappuccino," she says in admiration, not an ounce of bitchyness, I swear. She and I both fully know and appreciate the value of being able to sit - with a cappa - alone - as a mother. I immediately relax, laugh, and give her a reassuring smile, "please don't worry, I've been there!" I giggle.

Whilst I may look like I'm in an easier stage of life, the truth is, I'm stuck at a quarter to getting my shit together. You know, when you feel like it's coming together but isn't quite there yet.

I pick up a strip of sugar and take a moment to read the quote printed on the side of the packaging.

"A bright future beckons. The onus is on us, through hard work, honesty and integrity, to reach for the stars" - Nelson Mandela.

It's with this that I feel the sudden desire to reflect on the current chapter of my life.

In my thirties, I can comfortably say I have learned a lot. I had both my kids by then, experienced the aftermath of loss, been through the fires of a global pandemic, and started two successful businesses - albeit one collapsed upon said pandemic. The other sprouted from said pandemic. What is that thing 'they say': when one door closes, another opens. Well, this bell rang profoundly true at that point in my life.

I had witnessed and personally experienced the undeniable reality of women blatantly putting other women down. There was no real fortuitous overwhelming spread of girls' clubs on my journey, unlike the inevitable boy's clubs forming at every Padel and golf location in the city.

Not that I have anything against either of these sports. In fact, I happen to have a very pretty pink tartan golf bag and matching clubs. Not that I play much. I was also recently gifted a rather cute bag for my Padel gear, which I do actually play. And surprisingly, love. I'm not the best - but I can mostly hit the ball across the net.

Still, in my thirties, I embraced #momlife - I'm a class mom 6 years running, assist in the PTA, have the coaches on WhatsApp, and am the go-to for the general "what's happening at school this week" kinda of questions. I guess, since I left my pretty cushy and rather successful corporate life when I was just 29, I got my OCD organisational fix through school activities and socialising. Being the mom to volunteer to welcome new parents happily, set up play dates, and, well, just keep trying to live up to this self-inflicted delusion of an unattainable ideal.

I went from wondering how some moms could be in gym gear all day every day to being the mom who actively tries and mostly fails to wear gym gear every day. An underrated clothing attire, in my opinion, is black leggings. I've tried and tested many types and have finally tracked down the best fit, best fabric, and least sports-looking type. Which is ideal for someone who isn't visually categorised as a "gym bunny."

So, if you happen to see me around with black leggings - just know I'm in mom mode. Don't mess with my kids. Don't judge me. Chances are I'm enjoying my peanut butter cup smoothie and would rather be left alone.

I'd hit rock bottom financially and mentally, lost weight, and gained more. Still on that mission to lose more. Seems like it's my never-ending story. I've never been one of those I'll-eat-whatever-I-want-and-won't-get-fat kinda people. I'm more in denial of my true weight persona, which turns out to be an ill-have-another-slice-of-that-butter-cream-cake-and-a-full-cream-latte kinda gal.

I started meditating, and then I stopped. Found it hard to turn my brain off for a limited period of time. I realised my mind is like a browser with 50 tabs open; 6 are frozen, 2 are lagging, and I have no idea where the music is coming from.

I finally began to stop others from having the power to make me feel bad about myself or things or people in my life. Thanks to my husband, I have that constant reminder not to let people get me down with sly comments or even slyer tactics. If you're reading this, and you feel a sense of guilt - then know for sure - I'm talking about you.

I found the magical world of almost guilt-free luxury adult-only holidays. I've indulged in the most exquisite travel experiences and bought a few magnets along the way.

I'm about to turn 39, and as I ponder on whether this chapter will lead to my next book or not, I have a little voice inside me whispering, "fucking go for it." And on this note, I can't help but wonder if this is just my way of finding forty.

Chapter 2

Welcome To The Circus.

Those Are My Monkeys

So, I had survived the adventure of having one child and eventually found myself staring down the barrel of the sequel. Sure, having been through 4 years of uterus and sperm checkups, specialist doctor visits, disappointments, pregnancy testing, ovulation tracking, counting, etc.. nothing could have prepared me for what I was signing up for. The second child is like that unexpected ending of a movie you thought you had predicted well. But there I was, about to dive back into the madness with all the enthusiasm of a sleep-deprived psychopath. It's as if I was replaying the original plot, but only now have I got the extended director's cut with added scenes and never-before-seen footage.

The fact is that our first child pretty much traumatised us with her colic, her tendency to choke on my breastmilk flow, and her perpetual need for us to dance her off to lalaland every time she was meant to sleep. Whether that was every 2,3,4,5 hours - it gradually became just a nightly routine. We had a special playlist, and usually, by song 4, she was sound asleep. Till 5 am, that is.

So when our second daughter arrived, she was slightly different and seemed a bit more put-together in her first few days; I excitedly thought, "wow, so this is my easy child."

God heard me.

God laughed.

Okay, okay, let's rewind to the hospital routine. I remember when I thought that my first time around this block was the peak of disarray, tears, and nerves. Oh, how naive I was. The second time is not just deja vu - it's a full-blown remix. It's the same whirlwind of hospital gowns and theatre lights, but now, at this point, I'm seasoned in the art of chaos, blood, and needles. However, there is something uniquely entertaining about being rolled into the same delivery room, only this time around, I'm wearing some minor battle scars from our firstborn's toddler years. Like when she sumo style slams into my face mid-sleep, leaving me with a loud "Ayyyeee!" swollen lip and a very whimpering reassurance that I am ok. In an attempt to not scar my little munchkin into thinking she somehow broke mommy.

Oh, and that's not all, folks! Brace yourself; aside from the sleepless nights, here comes the unsolicited advice 2.0. Both are back with a vengeance. If I ever thought I'd escape Aunt Petunia's lecture on the benefits of breastfeeding babies, not so fast there, Ally, think again. This time, the advice came with a side of "You know, the way I did it was..."

Gone are the days when my only concern was the size of my belly and my ridiculous cravings for popcorn and rum & raisin ice cream. The second time around, my feet were swollen like overripe mangos, and I had built a career that demanded more from me than ever before. Adding to the mix is the social calendar of our first child, which had somehow morphed into a socialite-level schedule of 'My kid seems cooler than me.'

Okay, fine, the truth is that I do have a habit of RSVPing to every birthday party, and I do sign Abby up for various extra mural activities. So when we're facing the weekend ahead with three birthday parties and a family lunch in between, I can practically sense my husband's 'Bombastic side-eye' look before he even takes a peek at the calendar, silently questioning why on earth we're doing this. Well, I'll tell you why-honeypie: because if I don't do it, who will? How else is our little one supposed to blossom into the social butterfly I know she's destined to be? And let's not forget, I'm making sure she gets the opportunities I never dreamed of at her age. Ariel yoga, Acro dancing, and mindfulness weren't exactly part of my childhood repertoire!

In between all the dancing about, I also had a new baby to care for. That included what felt like 50,000 diaper changes, pumping myself like the cow god made me into (size and milk-related at that point), and, to top it off, almost no sleep.
It's a sure recipe for what some call 'losing-your-shit'. It's where any help is always welcome. Though the offers seem to dwindle once you have your second child - You somehow find yourself asking your 4-year-old to help you with some assistance for a diaper disaster that had your hands and bed covered in liquidy yellowish poo.

"Darling, Abby, please can you hand me some toilet paper as I've run out of wipes?" I say as calmly as I can, without making the baby or Abby feel like this is a horrific situation to be in. Which it was.

Abby, then 4 years old, brings me one square piece of toilet paper. Just one little square. I remember thinking, 'are you joking?' there is literally poo everywhere! But then my heart started to flutter, and eventually, it burst with love and pride. Her innocence and sweet intention to help were so pure, and I couldn't have been prouder. As it turns out, I survived the Poo-Extravaganza of 2018, I made it out alive, as did my curtains. The fact is, Abby will always go down as one of the best big sisters ever - even if it's one square of toilet paper at a time.

Playdates are no longer a simple affair; they're almost full-blown events with RSVPs, planned activities, and a variation of meal preps to cater to every new allergy and parental preference. Ballet recitals are now prepared for major productions, complete with glitter, tulle, crazy stage moms, and a parade of pint-sized prima donnas with winged eyeliner. And don't even get me started on the music and drama classes. What was once a casual sing-along wearing a long blonde plat wig is now a dramatic interlude of "Mom, she's better than me" for the best performance of "Let it go".

The school dress-up days are the cherry on top of this already overflowing sundae. If you ever thought dressing up one child was a mission? Try coordinating accessories, looks, and outfit options for two fashion-forward girls while juggling a full-time job and a house that's slowly turning into a battleground of rainbow-high dolls and misplaced socks.

*Oh god (note to self), remember to buy more socks *

With each new event and activity - my brain felt like it was running out of space.

We all have our own individual journeys when it comes to parenthood. It's probably the hardest job in the world - being a parent. Whilst we are on our own roads to raising our young, we definitely have a few consistencies that overlay each unique experience. Starting with the gross amount of pressure we offload on ourselves to be the best, do the best, and really make the best kids.

When you have one kid, you tend to be a bit of an overachiever. Attending every prenatal class, reading every parenting book cover-to-cover. You are fully entrenched in the parenting Olympics. But by the time baby number two arrives, let's be real - survival becomes the new gold medal. You'll likely develop ninja-like skills in the diaper-changing arena whilst comforting a very emotional toddler who happened to lose a tiny piece of a Happy Meal toy that really means nothing to anyone. Other than her in that very moment, because, truth be told, give the kid a new toy (even from trusty McD's), and it's like nothing ever existed before.

This, my friends, is called the parenting Olympics. Where multitasking should be categorised as an Olympic sport. With one kid, you are likely fully entrenched in a tag team marathon with your partner. With two kids, the tag-you're-it is no longer an opportunity to 'take a break' or 'catch a nap'. No sirry. Those are but legends of the past at this stage. With two, it's about team tactics, where one parent handles bedtime duty, whilst the other tackles bathtime duty. It's when one is serving dinner, whilst the other is helping with devices, all while reminding our little treasures to 'chew' and not just stare at the screens in zombie mode. When one is helping with a water rocket project, whilst the other is building Barbie's dream castle. It's like running a relay race and never quite feeling like you're crossing the finishing line.

OH, and don't forget to feed the dogs.

Having multiple kids is not for the faint of heart. However, if you are faint-hearted by nature, the second kid will whip you into shape before you can say, "hand me the wine."
However, whilst we aim for daily survival, I have to admit that having the second child changed my life. Where I struggled through my stint of severe postpartum depression and anxiety - now I am stronger because of it. Where I historically wouldn't be able to digest the idea of leaving my kids for a weekend away - now I'm happy to leave them with my mom and jet off to Istanbul for a week. Where I used to sleep on the edge of my kid's toddler bed just so she could 'touch feets' before she fell asleep - now I'm able to sit up right next to her and be honest with her that I will actually leave her side when she's asleep to go to my own bed. I used to wash the dummy every time it touched the floor, but now, admitting the 5-second rule is actually a 15-second rule and saying things like "you'll be alright" more frequently than I'd ever said before.

As the girls get a bit older, sure, things get a bit easier, especially once you stop getting summoned to wipe bums. However, generally speaking, girls tend to come with an innate sense of drama and sass that I'd like to think they didn't inherit from me. Albeit, we all know the truth - I'm all about the drama. There is nothing quite like being schooled by a miniature, sassier, and smarter version of yourself, usually in the form of the infamous second child.

"How is everyone today?" I ask

"I don't know, we're not everyone!" My 6-year-old responds.

I don't recall having the kahoonas to talk back to my mom when I was 6. I did grow some when I got older, though, especially around the 15-year-old mark.

I suddenly feel a mild sense of fear, knowing full well that I have 2 daughters. I was a total cow to my mum in adolescence. Karma is real, and I'm fucked.

They say that when you have one kid, you have just one kid. However, they also say that when you have two kids, it's like having twenty kids. Honestly speaking, it's not quite as bad as twenty kids. It's more like three kids because it's at this point that you usually realise the incompetencies your husband then displays. It starts when he feels like he needs to fight for your attention. With three so-called dependants on you, it's no longer an even 50% of your attention being split. Now, it's divided three ways between your two kids and him. It's truly a juggling act and requires a lot of patience and, truth be told, sometimes medication.

Just when I thought I'd mastered the art of multitasking, I realised that the second child came with a deluxe package of extras I didn't quite order. Of course, the lack of a manual for this upgrade meant we were left navigating this new territory with the grace of koalas on ice skates. The second child's arrival isn't just a continuation of the first chapter; it's a whole new book with its own set of unexpected plot twists. Like a real rollercoaster ride - in a whole new and exciting Adventureland theme park. Lookout for the welcome sign, it will read:

"Welcome to the sequel, where chaos is the new norm. Enjoy."

Chapter 3

Finding love

Swipe Left on Logic, Right on Feels

A h, love - the four-letter word that's responsible for countless sleepless nights, endless tubs of ice cream, and an unhealthy obsession with rom-coms that suggest you might just meet your soulmate after accidentally spilling coffee on them. Spoiler alert: if you spill coffee on someone, they're more likely to send you a dry-cleaning bill than a bouquet of roses. But let's not burst too many bubbles just yet. After all, hope is the fuel that powers the love train, right up until it derails in a fiery blaze of heartbreak and questionable life choices. Too doom and gloom? Perhaps.

They say that when you fall in love, you fall with your heart and not your head. This, dear reader, is precisely where the trouble begins. It's as if someone handed us a roadmap to relationship bliss and then swapped out the logical GPS with a faulty compass that only points to 'Bad Decisions

Avenue.' You know, the place where you can't help but repeat every romantic misstep your mother warned you about, and her mother warned her about, and so on.

As I sit here, musing about the absurdity of it all, I can't help but worry about my daughters. If I could turn back time, I'd go back to my own youthful days and hand myself a well-deserved slap across the face every time I made a romantic decision based on a fluttery heart rather than a clear head. But alas, time travel isn't a thing yet, so I'll have to settle for imparting my hard-earned wisdom in the hope that they don't repeat my mistakes.

The thing is, when you're young, the dating pool is like an all-you-can-eat buffet. The options seem endless, and the world is your oyster. You sift through this metaphorical ocean of potential partners with the naïveté of someone who's never experienced a seafood allergy. Blissfully unaware that some of those shiny oysters may be hiding a rather unpleasant surprise. But hey, you've got to kiss a few frogs to find your prince, right? Or so the fairy tales would have you believe. Truth be told, some frogs are just frogs, and no amount of kissing will change that. But then, something strange happens. As the years roll by, the dating pool starts to shrink. It's like the end of the buffet when the kitchen's closed, and all that's left is the wilted salad and questionable chicken. You've gone from dining at a Michelin-starred restaurant to picking over McDonald's and KFC. That's when you realise that maybe, just maybe, you should have been a bit more discerning when the buffet was fully stocked.

Enter Tinder, Bumble, and all the other dating apps that promise to deliver love to your doorstep with the convenience of a pizza delivery. These platforms are like the fast food of romance: quick, easy, and ultimately unsatisfying. Sure, you can swipe right and take your chances, but deep down, you know that the chances of true love hiding behind a profile pic probably aren't high. Also, rumour has it that these apps have evolved into notorious booty call apps. Which is a different type of 'connection', one that isn't quite relevant to this chapter. So, moving along...

As we age, understanding love becomes less like falling head over heels and more like appreciating a fine wine. In our youth, we're perfectly content with a bottle of something vaguely red that could double as a paint stripper. We didn't know better, and we didn't care. But as we grow older, our tastes refine. We start paying attention to things like texture, viscosity, and origin. We develop a discerning palate, recognising the difference between a full-bodied cabernet and a "bargain bin special."

Love, as it turns out, is much the same. We used to be drawn to the flashiest bottle on the shelf, not realising it might leave us with a raging hangover the next morning. As time went on, we learned to savour the experience, appreciating the subtle nuances that make a relationship truly remarkable. We started looking for depth, character, and that elusive quality known as - compatibility -something that wasn't even on our radar when we were simply trying to avoid dating a total psycho.

But here's the thing about wine (and love): it's never too late to develop a taste for the finer things. Sure, the dating pool might be more like a kiddie pool by the time you're in your late thirties, but that doesn't mean you can't find someone truly exceptional. It just means you need to be more selective.

You've earned the right to be picky, so why settle for anything less than a vintage worth savouring?

So, to my daughters and to anyone else who's still holding out hope for love - I say this: Don't rush it. Don't let your heart lead you down the rabbit hole without consulting your brain first. Love is a marathon, not a sprint, and it's perfectly okay to take your time. Because when you finally do find that one special person, it's going to be worth every sleepless night, every bad date, and every questionable decision you ever made.

<u>So you found love?</u>
Fast forward to having found your 'one', is the famous concept of loving your partner unconditionally. It's the stuff that oozes out of self-help books, shared as inspirational posts across your social media feed, and sometimes, these are the wise words placed upon us by our elders or people who are happily married. Or so we're told. But let's be real for a moment, shall we? Loving someone unconditionally is a lot like going gluten-free: It sounds virtuous and makes you look good in theory, but in practice, it's a whole lot harder than you expected.

I mean, let's start with the word "unconditional." It's almost as intimidating as "intermittent fasting," isn't it? The idea that you should love someone without any conditions whatsoever is enough to make even the most devoted partner uncertain of what that could entail. Because, let's face it, there are some pretty reasonable conditions to consider in any relationship, like not leaving wet towels on the bed, or a more recent frustration, perhaps, when they forget an important family lunch and accidentally double book themselves for another round of golf that's apparently impossible to get out of.

But, despite certain conditions we secretly deal with, there's something universally appealing about the idea of unconditional love. It's that pure, undiluted form of affection we're told to strive for, where you love someone no matter what, through thick and thin, good and bad, 'til death do you part or until you disagree about whether pineapple belongs on pizza (it doesn't, by the way).

So, how does one achieve this level of love? Is it even possible?

Achieving this level of love is about recognising that your partner is a flawed human being, just like you, and loving them despite (and sometimes because of) those flaws. It's about accepting that their annoying quirks and habits are part of the package, much like how you tolerate the queues at Zara for their end-of-season sale. You wish they weren't there, but you deal with it because you know the sale is worth it.

The fact is that nobody is perfect. And when you're in a long-term relationship, those imperfections have a way of becoming more noticeable over time.

I swear men are innately developed to have selective hearing.

"Don't forget to pick up my sister from the airport"

...

...

"Hello?"

"Hey babe"

So, what superpower did we score in relationships?

Well, my friends, we get the art of selective memory. It's our incredible ability to forget the little things that drive us bat shit crazy while focusing on the qualities that made you fall in love in the first place. It's the real trick to loving unconditionally - training our brains to gloss over minor annoyances. Always trying to remember the bigger picture.

After all, and I'll say it again, nobody's perfect, including you.

Now, let's address the elephant in the room: being in love doesn't mean putting up with anything and everything. There's a fine line between loving someone unconditionally and enabling unhealthy behaviour. If your partner is doing something that's genuinely harmful to you, to themselves, or to the relationship - then that's not something to be ignored or embraced.

It definitely isn't about sacrificing your own well-being for the sake of the relationship. It's about supporting each other, lifting each other up, and making each other better people. If your partner is doing something that crosses the line from "quirk" to "problem," it's okay to set boundaries. Loving unconditionally doesn't mean loving without limits. It means loving with wisdom and discernment.

Every relationship will face its share of challenges, and it's during these times that your commitment to unconditional love will be tested. Maybe it's a big fight, a financial crisis, or a health scare. Whatever the challenge, these moments are when you find out what your love is really made of. It's easy to love someone when everything is going well. But when the going gets tough, that's when unconditional love really shines. It's about choosing to stay and work things out, even when it would be easier to walk away. It's about finding a way to reconnect, even when you feel like you're on opposite sides of the planet. It's about always coming back to love, even after a fight. It's about forgiving your partner (and yourself) when things don't go the way you anticipated. It's about saying, "I'm sorry," even when you don't want to. Because at the end of the day, it's not about being right; it's about being together. It's a kind of love that goes beyond the surface. It's the kind of love that lasts, not because it's perfect, but because it's real and it's yours.

You build a partnership that's based on trust, respect, and mutual admiration. And that, in fact, is worth more than a lifetime supply of gluten-free cookies.

So, the next time you're tempted to get annoyed at your partner for something trivial, take a step back. Remember why you fell in love with them in the first place. And choose to love them unconditionally. After all, true love isn't about finding someone who's perfect; it's about finding someone who's perfect for you.

And if they happen to be perfect at doing the dishes, well, then that's just a bonus.

Chapter 4

From tequila shots to bedtime socks.

When Comfort Trumps Clubbing.

Surely, it was a mere five minutes ago - or so it feels - that I was the reigning queen of cool. Without uttering the famous "back in my day" words. I was the one who could secure VVIP passes to the hottest parties. The one who orchestrated nights out with the girls that ended with us dancing our hearts out to Beyoncés latest mixes - totally tipsy and with not a care in the world. The one who used to be on the dance floor whilst the club was preparing to close with their inevitable play of some obscure song like the Gummie Bears theme song. My legs were indefatigable; they danced straight through the drunk with minimal sweat. Those were the days when I could down tequila like it had a taste other than 'yuck' and still emerge standing as though I was a well-oiled machine made of embellished shoes and youthful exuberance. What surprises me more than anything about my antics back then is that I would want to party every weekend if I could.

• • •

So there I was, a mere 38 years old, enjoying my age-appropriate social vibe of dinner and wine with adultier adults. Which is code for, people already in their 40's. I'd recently started improving my wine education and actually had a preferred type. It was a new level of sophistication that only reminded me that I was heading in one direction, starting with an O and ending in a DUH! (Older)

Regardless, as I was browsing through the wine list, I realised that I had evolved from the simple "I'll have a glass of house white" or "just the house red for me, please." I noticed they had options on my favourite blends of Chenin Blanc. Great, I thought - just be cool and choose one... anyone.

However, as I was debating which option to choose, almost an eenie-meenie-miny-mo situation - the prices caught my eye. One glass of Chenin Blanc was approximately R149. However, a bottle of the same blend was R379.

Now, I'm no expert, but my basic math told me to go for the bottle. Obviously, I do not anticipate drinking more than perhaps two glasses as that's usually my threshold before laughs become exceptionally loud and conversations looser. I did figure there would be someone else in my dinner group who would probably join in on this bottle, and it would work out quite economical, actually. I was proud of my forward-thinking.

Needless to say, all the seats at this table opted for anything but a white wine. Mostly red, which I hear is a more sophisticated choice. Perhaps I will indulge in that pallet when I'm 40. Let's see.

So, feeling a little sheepish for having just ordered a bottle, I went with the flow with my first glass. As the night went on, the conversation was a rich concoction of anything from the riots in London to the next adult trip. Ironically, it was agreed that I would be in London next year in September in honour of my looming 40th birthday.

The hostess at the restaurant was incredibly kind and welcoming. I thought, "Wow, this is how a business thrives with incredible staff that takes good care of their customers." She went on to explain that they make their own tequila and offered us a taster.

Tequila was not something I opted for since entering my 30s. It always had a weird, nauseating reminder of my youth associated with it. Regardless, as she was so lovely, I agreed to try a taste. It was actually a full-size shot glass, but surprisingly, it was the best tequila I'd ever, ever had. Definitely did not take me back to that night in varsity at that club when I puked out the Olmeca right on the pavement. In retrospect, I have to thank my lucky stars that not many people noticed my faux pas. Generally speaking, it was moments like this that truly traumatised me from wanting tequila ever again.

As the night went on, I enjoyed the most divine salmon on a bed of pea and mint risotto as a main and tasted a few shared tapas, including some calamari and prawns. Very much my type of food - modern Mediterranean. Seeing as how it was mostly seafood I indulged in, the Chenin Blanc was going down quite nicely. That first glass almost skipped the bitter phase and went straight into the 'oh, this tastes like juice' phase.

Just then, I saw our waitress glide by, effortlessly topping up everyone's glasses. It was like a revelation moment, one of those times when everything suddenly clicked into place; no wonder my glass wasn't dipping, and no wonder the taste was evolving. I looked at the bottle in the ice bucket on the small table next to me. For a moment, I thought, 'It couldn't be'. Trues bob, it was! I had drunk 80% of the bottle aced out.

The sudden realisation had me questioning my ability to survive. Was I really ok? Was I talking at a reasonable level? Did my conversation change? OH Fuck.

I was 100% pure dronk. Not drunk. Dronk.

The kind of drunk where vowels stretch out longer than they should, where the room starts spinning just slightly, and where the line between thought and speech becomes dangerously thin.

The journey home was a blur, but not the kind you can chalk up to a pleasant buzz. No, this was the kind of blur that had me gripping the door handle of the car with pale-knuckled intensity. My husband, the saint that he is, was driving us home. The ride felt endless; every curve in the road was a fresh assault on my already churning stomach. I was desperately trying to hold it together, mentally coaching myself through each breath, but I could feel it coming, that inevitable wave of nausea. And then, there was no holding back.

The first vomit struck mid-journey in the car. My poor husband barely had time to pull over before I lost control. The once pristine interior of our car was now ground zero. I remember the look on his face, part concern, part horror, and a sliver of resignation. He knew this wasn't over, and so did I.

When we finally got home, I stumbled out of the car, the cool night air hitting me like a slap. I made it as far as the garden before round two hit. This time, I was prepared, or as prepared as one can be in such a state. I leaned over the nearest patch of grass and let it all out. Or so I thought. The garden, once my peaceful sanctuary, was now the scene of my humiliation. I could barely stand, but I managed to drag myself towards the house, hoping that the worst was behind me.

But the wine had other plans. No sooner had I made it inside than I was hit again. I barely made it to the bathroom in time for round three. My legs felt like jelly, and the tiles beneath me felt colder and harder than ever before. I was starting to think this was some sort of karmic retribution for enjoying myself too much. I mean, who did I think I was ordering a bottle of wine like that?

But it wasn't over. Oh no, the wine had one final parting shot. I tried to settle myself on the couch, just for a moment's peace, but my stomach wasn't done yet. Round four happened right there in the living room, on a rug I particularly liked. I could almost hear the rug crying out in protest as I emptied the last of my stomach's contents onto it. I was too far gone to even care at that point.

The silver lining? I was certain I must have lost half my body weight from the ordeal.

But, alas, fate has a way of kicking you when you're down. After what felt like an eternity of retching, I finally gathered myself and fell fast asleep. The next morning, I mustered up the strength to weigh myself. I don't know why I did it; maybe I wanted some small consolation for my suffering. Some tangible evidence that this whole night wasn't for nothing. I stepped onto the scale, closed my eyes, and waited for the numbers to appear.
When I finally opened them, I stared in disbelief. Not a single Kilo lost. Not a gram. I had gone through all that, four rounds of gut-wrenching misery, and my body had the audacity to hold onto every last bit of weight.

So there you have it. The night, I overindulged and emerged on the other side with absolutely nothing to show for it except a killer hangover and a story that would be too embarrassing if it weren't so absurd. Sometimes, the universe just loves to keep us humble.

So, having been through 'one of those nights' at this age, heading towards 40 felt even more like an inner turmoil epiphany. I found myself reminiscing about how I viewed my parents at this age. To me, they were practically relics from a bygone era, not quite the type with sensible shoes and early bedtimes. But regardless, they were old.

But here I am, navigating the uncharted waters of my late 30s, grappling with the fact that my wild party days are now legendary tales of the past. Even if they weren't, they definitely weren't intentional and most definitely not well managed. Once upon a time, I could bounce back from a night out with little more than a groggy morning and a greasy breakfast. But now, the after-effects seem to linger, clinging to me like an unwelcome guest. The resilience I once took for granted has been replaced by a fragility that's hard to ignore. In my 20s, hangovers were badges of honour, proof that I had lived fully and freely. I'd laugh them off, reliving the highlights with friends as we nursed our sore heads. But now, a hangover isn't just a physical ailment; it's a full-blown existential introspection. It's the universe's way of reminding me that I'm not as young as I used to be, that my body isn't the same and that maybe, just maybe, it's time to start acting my age. But what does that even mean, acting my age? I never imagined myself as someone who would have to choose between a glass of wine and a good night's sleep, but here we are. The truth is, aging isn't just about the physical changes, though those are certainly there. It's also about the mental and emotional shifts, the subtle (and sometimes not-so-subtle) ways in which our priorities realign. Nights that once ended with last calls and loud music now more often conclude with a warm bath and a book. And you know what? I'm more than okay with that.

However, that doesn't mean there isn't a very small part of me that mourns the loss of the carefree, wild nights of my youth. Those nights were filled with spontaneity and with the kind of joy that only comes from being young and not having to worry too much about the consequences. But life changes, and so do we. I've had to embrace the fact that my body can't handle what it used to and that my mind no longer craves chaos. Instead, I find myself seeking out peace, quiet, and a sense of stability - exactly what I used to scoff at.

So, as I sat there nursing the aftermath of a night that got away from me, I was reminded that aging is a process, not a destination. It's about learning to let go of who you were and making peace with who you're becoming.

Those party days from my 20s feel like ancient history. They are more like myths than memories. It's as if I'm looking at my past through a sepia filter, while the present feels like I'm starring in a sitcom called "How Did I End Up Here?"

Teaser: I'm always in bed by 9:30 PM, tucked in, with warm feet and a stomach full of something decidedly not tequila.

The transition from high heels to house slippers is less of a gradual change and more of a jarring, sudden shift. These days, Saturday nights are more likely to feature a riveting marathon of an addictive Netflix series rather than a gathering of any sort.

Conversations are now healthy, intellectual, and juicy reports of Love is Blind, the UK version.

We focus on enjoying the little things and making time for coffee dates. Because even though life is busy and time is tight. Socialising now is more comfortable. Albeit, whilst we claim rank and embrace #momlife - We're so busy playing hide-and-seek with Father Time that we've turned aging into a full-time job. We shell out enough anti-aging treatments to fund a small island, all in the name of youth. But here's the catch: while we're laser-zapping, injecting, and wrinkle-smoothing, we're actually speeding up the very thing we're trying to avoid. Who knew the fountain of youth came with a side of irony?

The way I see it is that the world is just getting younger as we get older. So technically, we're like the generation that never ages.

Remember this one for future banter with Gen Z.

Am I worried?

Hell no, I couldn't be happier. I love my age-appropriate sense of humour and my obsession with comfort. The DJ booth has been replaced by a couch, the dance floor by a rug, and the tequila shots with chamomile tea. And while I may not be enjoying the club anymore, I'm certainly reigning supreme in my cozy kingdom.

And it's incredible.

Chapter 5

A Mental Health Odyssey

Now More Popular Than Kale

As I settle into my psychiatrist's typically overly comfortable chair, I'm compelled to confront my own personal experiences at a level I'm not very good at, to be honest. I find that because I'm so busy keeping up with, well, keeping up - that the tiny nuances of my own existence go unnoticed. I, therefore, sit on this rather comfy recliner and sound more demented than I actually am.

"How is your mood?" she asks.

My mind immediately shifts gear and tries to recall what 'mood' even means. Is it the bad mood I was in with Roux because he didn't get the pool sorted after asking multiple times? Or is it the good mood I was in when my quick trip to the shops had me winning at some epic sales? Well, it's neither. She wanted to know generally how my mood had been over the last 3 months. And all I can think of is how I can't quite remember what I had for breakfast. Did I even have breakfast?

"It's been good", I respond nonchalantly.

"On a scale of 1-10?" she probes.

Don't say 5, I repeat in my mind! That sounds like I'm neither here nor there. 6 sounds average. 4 sounds problematic. 8 sounds a bit too happy. So, 7 seemed like a reasonable response.

I've come a long way down this mental health road. It wasn't all smooth sailing either. When it was first suggested to me that I see a specialist, my immediate reaction was, "no, fuck you. You don't know me. This is who I am".

It took four visits to four different psychiatrists - with me judging each of them more every time. It was the fourth consult that kinda led somewhere, albeit I was tricked into going.

I was 8 weeks postpartum, and saying I hadn't slept is by no means an exaggeration. I would literally watch the sunrise daily. In retrospect, I can admit that it was a pretty bad time for me. Not referencing my angel baby. But rather, it was my undeniable crazy, which I was blind to.

So after some counselling from my nearest and dearest - I was promised two nights of sleep if I just went into the hospital, to which I agreed. The idea of some sleep didn't sound too bad.

The plan was for my mom to come up to stay and help with the kids whilst I slept. It was only when I was fully admitted and after waiting hours to speak to psychiatrist number four. Did she tell me I may not go home for two days?

They lied!

I was livid - this was exactly why I didn't want to do this in the first place. My brain was fluctuating between the worry that I'd got to get back to my baby and the deeply ingrained desire for what was promised to me: sleep. That is all—no time for this fluffy mumbo jumbo. Gimme my sleep and let me go, I wanted to shout.

So, as I sat contemplating the deceit of it all and already regretting every step that led me here, the nurse came in. She was calm, cool, and collected - totally unfazed by the fact that I was one sleepless night away from staging a personal protest. She casually handed me my prescription medication like it was a cup of coffee, as if these little pills were the magical solution to all my problems.
God, wouldn't that be great!

I didn't trust her. Not one bit. The second she left the room, I slipped the meds into my bag, feeling like I was in some scene from that old movie Girl Interrupted. Except instead of an angsty 90s teen, I was a frazzled, sleep-deprived mom who hadn't had a moment of peace since the epidural had worn off 8 weeks prior.

The rest of the night, I lay in bed, staring at the ceiling. The hospital room was eerily quiet, and the clock's ticking started to feel like some kind of cruel joke. I didn't sleep a wink. But hey, at least I wasn't drugged into zombie mode, right?

The next morning, the doctor breezed in again with her clipboard and professional detachment. "How did you sleep?" she asked like we were discussing the weather.

"Terribly," I said, resisting the urge to cry. I hadn't been this tired since... well, since the night before.

Without missing a beat, she nodded thoughtfully as if this was the most interesting news she'd heard all day. "We'll have to up your dosage then."

I nearly choked. "Up" the dosage? Lady, I didn't even take the first one!

It was at that moment I realised this whole experience wasn't like Girl Interrupted at all. Because I wasn't the rebellious teenager fighting the system. I was a 'mom interrupted'. Managing to sneak around my own mental health care while trying to be some version of sane. Just trying to survive the chaos while pretending I had it all under control.

Sheepishly, I had to admit that I didn't take the pill from the night before because I simply didn't trust her. She seemed unbothered by this mild insult. She shrugged off my comment, like she'd heard it before, and simply asked me to please take the medicine today.

Trues Bob, I took the med that night and slept like the baby I wished I was at the time.

Moral of this story, dear reader?
Sleeping like a baby is an ironic saying. Babies don't sleep. Moms on meds do.

The fact is that mental health conversations have changed dramatically. In today's world, there's a certain acceptance surrounding mental health that wasn't always there. Ten years ago, if you admitted you were seeing a psychiatrist, people might have looked at you like you were one step away from a padded room. Today, though? It's almost like talking about your latest yoga class. Mental health care has become trendy in a way, but not in the dismissive sense, more in the "self-care is as important as skincare" kind of way.

Now, don't get me wrong. Even with this newfound openness, there's still a lingering awkwardness in admitting you need help. That whole "I'm fine, everything's fine, look how fine I am" charade we keep up is hard to shake. Especially as we get older, when the balancing act between career and kids gets more complicated.

I've said it before, and I'll say it again. The closer you get to 40, the more you start to accept that it's okay not to have it all figured out. You realise that perfection is overrated, and so is pretending to have your life together when you're clearly hanging on by a thread. This isn't just some epiphany that comes with age, though. It's a slow realisation that hits when you're trying to remember why you walked into the kitchen or when you're Googling "types of Padel rackets" at 2 am. instead of sleeping like a normal person.

You get to a point where you stop apologising for needing help and start owning it because you've been through the wringer, and damn it, you're still standing.

In today's world, mental health care is seen as part of the self-love toolkit. Therapy, meditation apps, and mindfulness are all part of the same conversation. Protecting this toolkit is of the utmost importance. Don't let negative Nancy try to bring you down with their doom and gloom. You need to guard your inner peace. So the next time someone answers, "how are you?" With "oh, I'm alive" - give them a polite nod, but know that you're working on a higher frequency. You've got more important things to do than merely 'exist.'

The good news is that the associated stigma to mental health has begun to fade, and with it, the need to hide your struggles. Truth is, it has become like the rest of adulting. It's one more thing you add to the to-do list, like buying groceries or getting the gas refilled. You just accept it. And the best part? No one's judging you for it anymore (well, at least not the people that matter). It's about knowing yourself well enough to say, "I can't do this alone, and that's okay."

By the time you hit 40, mental health acceptance isn't just a personal win; it's a societal one. The world might still be a bit chaotic, but at least we're all in it together, swapping therapist recommendations like they're recipes for the best-seeded loaf.

Chapter 6

Career Menopause

The Unplanned Rebrand

After years in the advertising trenches, I'd become a maestro of client service. My life revolved around appeasing clients, exceeding their expectations, and mastering the fine art of saying, "Absolutely, we can do that!" while internally wondering how on earth we would pull it off. My job was like being on call 24/7 for demanding, high-maintenance clients who loved to change their minds and occasionally throw tantrums. But, as any seasoned ad exec will tell you, it was all in a day's work until the pandemic hit and turned the entire industry into a scene from a disaster movie.

Suddenly, clients stopped paying, and my once-bustling agency began to resemble a ghost town, empty, echoey, and a little bit eerie. I found myself facing the unprecedented decision to liquidate my agency voluntarily. It was like deciding to end a long-term relationship, except instead of breaking up over dinner, I was doing it with spreadsheets and a tear-soaked coffee cup.

The thought of abandoning the world of advertising was both terrifying and exhilarating. On one hand, it was a familiar realm where I had built my career, honed my skills, and developed a vast array of marketing jargon that I could spout at parties. On the other hand, the idea of shifting gears entirely was like discovering a new hobby in your mid-30s and realising you're actually good at it. It was thrilling! I was handed a blank canvas and told, "Go wild!" without worrying about staying inside the lines.

This thrilling shift is what I've come to refer to as "Career Menopause." Just like the biological version, it involves a sudden and unanticipated change, complete with its own set of mood swings and hot flushes, except instead of fluctuating hormones, it's fluctuating career paths. It's a time of reflection and reinvention, where you reassess what you really want to do, who you really want to be, and what to do with the mountains of accumulated branded office supplies that now seem like stale sample sale stock.

Career menopause is an unpredictable and chaotic stage, marked by a strange mix of fear and excitement. Fear because you have an opportunity to walk a path you've never walked before. Excitement because you have an opportunity to walk a path you've never walked before. You're faced with endless possibilities but also paralysed by the sheer volume of choices. Do I become a freelance consultant, a yoga instructor, or maybe an artisanal cheese maker? The world is your oyster, but you're not quite sure if you have the right tools to open it.

As I navigated this new phase, I found myself reflecting on my old life with a mix of nostalgia and relief. No more 3 a.m. email crisis, no more endless client revisions, no more pretending that "buzzword compliance" is a real thing. Instead, I was embarking on a journey of self-discovery, armed with a portfolio of skills and a slightly battered ego.

In this career metamorphosis, every day felt like an episode of a reality TV show where I was both the contestant and the audience. There were moments of triumph, like discovering that I was surprisingly good at something new, and moments of doubt, like questioning whether I'd accidentally walked into a professional identity crisis. But through it all, I embraced the chaos with a sense of humour and an unwavering belief that, even in career menopause, reinvention is not only possible but also incredibly liberating.

So there I was, navigating the uncharted waters of a career transformation and loving every chaotic minute of it. The advertising world may have been my past, but the future is a blank page waiting for new ideas, new challenges, and maybe even a few new career paths. After all, if life's a journey, then career menopause is just a pit stop, a chance to recalibrate, refresh, and take on whatever comes next with a fresh perspective and a smile.

Enter Global Pandemic.

Without diving too deep into the global chaos that COVID-19 unleashed, I can confidently sit back and admit that the entire lockdown period feels like a blur. It's as if time bent, twisted, and reshuffled itself, leaving me with a hazy, dreamlike memory of what actually happened.

One moment, I was running a business, and the next, I was closing it down, only to find somehow myself launching a new one. The transition felt like a scene change in a play; one minute, the curtains were down, and when they lifted, I was in an entirely different act of life. And somewhere in between those acts, I managed to become a published author.

Seems like a lot, right? And yet, if you asked me to recount those days in detail, I'd struggle to piece together a coherent timeline. There are fragmented memories that pop up occasionally, like flashes of a strange dream, some of them vivid, others completely nonsensical. Let's start with the business I closed. It wasn't easy. Letting go of something I'd poured my heart and soul into was tough. But in those weirdly reflective lockdown days, I realised it was time to move on. I remember the empty office, the echo of the last chair scraping across the floor, and the click of the door as it closed behind me for the final time. It was bittersweet but mostly surreal. Then, because apparently, I'm a glutton for punishment, I decided to start a new business. Looking back, I'm not entirely sure what compelled me to take on such a challenge during a global pandemic. Maybe it was the endless supply of coffee or the desperate need for something, anything, to focus on other than the grim news headlines. Whatever it was, I threw myself into it with the same energy people were throwing flour into bread dough.

Oh, yes. The bread. If there's one thing I remember clearly, it's the bread. I became one of those people, those suddenly obsessed quarantine bakers who churned out loaves like it was going out of style. I'm talking about an absurd amount of bread. Sourdough, banana bread, you name it. I baked it. Was I any good at it? Debatable. But there was something oddly comforting about kneading dough and watching it rise. It felt like one small thing I could control in a world that had gone utterly off the rails.

And speaking of control, or the illusion of it, there was the whole toilet paper situation. Why toilet paper became the currency of the apocalypse is beyond me, but there I was, stockpiling rolls like they were bars of gold. There's something faintly ridiculous about it now, but at the time, it made perfect sense. If nothing else, I was going to be prepared for whatever came next, even if it was just a never-ending parade of Zoom meetings with a well-stocked bathroom.
Somehow, amidst all the baking, business ventures, and the great toilet paper fiasco, I also wrote a book. A whole book.

I'm still not entirely sure how I managed that, but I suppose there's something to be said for the strange bursts of creativity that can arise in times of crisis. Maybe it was a way to process everything that was happening, or perhaps it was just another way to escape the monotony of lockdown life. Whatever the case, the words flowed, and before I knew it, I had a manuscript. I'm not going to pretend it was all smooth sailing; there were days when the cursor blinked blankly at me for hours. But in the end, I did it.

Yet, despite the chaos, or maybe because of it, I found myself immersed in new ventures, new challenges, and new creations. I closed a chapter of my life, quite literally and figuratively, and opened a new one. There was loss, yes, but there was also growth.

And now, looking back, I can't help but wonder: how much of what we did during lockdown was a response to fear, a need to feel in control when everything felt out of control? Or was it simply a way to pass the time in a world that seemed to have pressed the pause button?

Whatever it was, it's over now. The world has moved on, and so have I. But every so often, when I catch a whiff of freshly baked bread or see an overflowing shelf of toilet paper, I'm reminded of that strange, blurry time. It was a period of confusion and clarity, loss and creation, endings and beginnings, all wrapped up in a fog that, even now, hasn't fully lifted.

Maybe one day, the memories will sharpen, and I'll be able to recount exactly what happened during those months. Or maybe they'll stay blurry, a testament to a time when the world and I - were in flux. Either way, it's a chapter of my life that I'll always carry with me, even if I can't quite put it all together.

Chapter 7

The Paradox of Motherhood

From Crayons to Crisis

Being a mother is a high-stakes job, and the job description reads: "Protect your children from every possible harm while letting them stumble through life's obstacles with grace and resilience." It sounds straightforward in theory: you shield them from the storm but let them learn from a few raindrops. In practice, though, it's a lot harder said than done. Motherhood is a paradox wrapped in lessons and sprinkled with a healthy dose of irony. From the moment that tiny human enters the world, you find yourself caught in the tension between protecting them from the world and preparing them to face it. You're their first line of defence and their biggest cheerleader, even when the world seems challenging.

In theory, the idea that kids need to experience minor hurts to grow up strong makes absolute sense. Life lessons come from falling off the proverbial bike, getting a little scraped up, and learning to dust oneself off.

However, the schoolyard is the ultimate testing ground for your protective instincts. It's like a gladiator arena for small people, where the stakes are high, and the rules are made up on the spot. You send your child out there with a kiss on the forehead and a pep talk about kindness, all the while knowing that you can't step in and fight their battles for them.

Your evenings are spent with introspective debates, trying to balance the scales of justice in your home. So, you channel your energy into crafting the perfect response, a blend of empathy, encouragement, and the occasional pep talk that may as well come with a gold star for good behaviour.

In the end, being a mother is about finding that delicate balance between protection and growth, a feat that's rarely executed without a few missteps and a fair amount of parental guilt.

●●●

As I unbuckled my youngest from her car seat, I declared, 'You're FREE!' She quickly corrected me, saying, 'No, I'm free and a half!' I couldn't help but giggle and pull her close for a snuggle. At that moment, I realised these precious little exchanges might not last forever, and many would likely fade from memory. But it wasn't just the boldness of her statement that made me giggle with pride. It was the admiration I felt for my three-and-a-half-year-old, standing her ground so comfortably, certain in her version of the truth.

Parenting is funny like that; it's a never-ending game of 'Which Way Is Up?' just when you think you've got a handle on things, your child hits you with a 'free and a half', and suddenly, you're reevaluating everything you thought you knew. It's in these small, seemingly insignificant moments that you realise you're raising a tiny human who's already mastering the art of negotiation and self-expression.

And let's be honest, as much as we like to believe we're the ones in charge, it's these little people who run the show. We're just here to make sure they don't eat crayons or declare 'chocolate for dinner!' every night. We may never know if we're 'doing it right,' but if they can stand firm in their beliefs, even if those beliefs include being 'free and a half', then maybe, just maybe, we're doing okay. After all, parenting isn't about perfection. It's about embracing the chaos, celebrating the small victories, and knowing that at the end of the day, you've managed to keep a tiny, stubborn human alive and thriving.

Motherhood is also about learning on both sides. Your child learns from you, and you, in turn, learn more about yourself and the world through them. It's a delicate dance of teaching and letting go, guiding and stepping back. One day, you're showing them how to tie their shoelaces, and the next, they're schooling you on the latest tech trend that you didn't even know existed. All whilst still trying to convince yourself that you are 'still cool'.

But the real learning happens in those unscripted moments when life doesn't go according to plan. It's in the times when your child faces a challenge that you can't solve with a band-aid or a reassuring hug. It's when they come home from school, eyes brimming with tears because they didn't get invited to a birthday party or didn't make the team. You learn that sometimes, all you can do is be there, listen, and resist the urge to fix everything. You learn that your child is more resilient than you ever imagined and that maybe you're a little tougher than you thought, too.

And while you're learning all of this, your child is watching you, soaking up the unspoken lessons. They see how you handle stress, how you react to setbacks, and how you navigate the ups and downs of life. They learn from your example, even when you're not at your best (which, let's face it, is more often than we'd like to admit).

Then, of course, there's the schoolyard circus, the place where all of your parenting theories are put to the test. The schoolyard is a microcosm of society, a place where social hierarchies are established, alliances are formed, and drama unfolds faster than you can say "break time."

It's here that your child will encounter the full spectrum of human behaviour, from the kindness of a friend who shares their lunch to the sting of a bully's taunt. And as much as you want to march onto that playground and set things right, you know that this is their arena, not yours. You can offer advice, dry their tears, and teach them how to stand up for themselves, but ultimately, they have to navigate the schoolyard circus on their own.

The paradox? While the schoolyard can be a place of challenges, it's also a place of growth. It's where your child will learn how to deal with conflict, how to make friends, and how to bounce back from disappointment. It's where they'll begin to understand that life isn't always fair, but that doesn't mean they can't find their own way through it.

Take, for instance, this scenario that unfolded - quite frankly, awakening the inner Selina Kyle in me. For those who aren't well versed in DC comic trivia, Catwoman is the alter ego of Selina Kyle. So whilst I hadn't quite reached the Catwoman stage of intensity. I was definitely lingering in her territory. It was a Sunday evening, and we were bang in the middle of that typical end of week downer. You know, when you walk around knowing you have to get stuff done in the upcoming week, but also knowing you can't quite start yet because it's technically still 'the weekend'. It's an ironic conundrum if you ask me.

I could sense some anxiety and nerves arising from Abby's aura. She was just 10 years old and was emitting a level of worry that I couldn't allow to go on.

"What's going on, Abby? Are you ok?" I asked with a warm and nurturing tone. Abby knew that there was nothing she couldn't tell me. It was something I had ingrained into her from the time she was a baby. I remind her all the time that I will always be there for her, and she must never be scared to tell me anything. Nothing would deteriorate the love I have for my babies. In turn, nothing would compromise the support I would offer them either.

Abby went on, after a bit of nudging, to explain that she really didn't want to go swimming the next day. She had worked herself up into such a state that repeated consolation was not working as quickly as I had hoped. It turns out the coach was being disrespectful, nasty, and just an absolute dickhead, if I can put it that way. Instead of encouraging the kids, he pinned their skills up against one another; he called individual kids out for not being fast enough, and he splashed the faces of those who struggled a little more than the others. He was tormenting these poor kids, and I wanted to ring his neck.

As Abby shared her fears and feelings, I felt my blood begin to boil. It was the kind of anger that made your vision go slightly red, your pulse slightly quicken, and your protective instincts kick into gear. And that's when I felt her – my inner Catwoman – not the elegant, sly villain, but the fierce, unapologetic protector who wouldn't let anything or anyone hurt those she loves. Words were springing to mind, and a lot of them were curse words. I was on the edge of doing something reckless, like sending off a very rude email to the school, which may not sound as reckless as the thought of storming into that pool the next day and teaching that coach a lesson in humility – claws out.

But instead of going all Gotham City vigilante right then and there, I took a deep breath, a slow exhale, and tried to reel in the impulse. I knew I had to be strategic. Abby didn't need a full-on spectacle at school with the stigma of having her mother complain to the school. What she needed was a role model who could show her how to handle these kinds of situations with grace and courage.

"I'm so sorry this happened, Abby. But guess what? We're going to fix it," I said, my voice steady, though my inner claws were itching for action. "That's not how coaches should be operating. Its not the norm and we will chat to the school about it."

The next morning, I didn't waste time. I called the school and set up a meeting with the principal and coach to address the toxic behaviour. As much as I wanted to march in, cape swirling behind me, and deliver justice, I knew the power of playing the long game. Words, after all, are mightier than claws.

Later that week, A new coach took over. Someone kind, encouraging, and focused on building confidence. At that moment, as I watched her smile return, I knew that sometimes being a hero isn't about a dramatic rescue but about quietly, fiercely making sure your loved ones are always safe and supported.

And while Selina Kyle would have slinked away into the night, I stayed proud and strong, teaching my daughter that she too can rise from the toughest of situations without losing her strength or her heart.

It's at this moment that I'm reminded of another iconic mother in Disney history. Cinderella's mom once told her young princess, "be kind and have courage." Words that I consider wise and worthy of constant repetition.

So, with this in mind, along with the following questions lingering: how do we survive the paradox of motherhood? How do we balance the urge to protect with the need to let them learn and grow? How do you survive the schoolyard circus without losing your mind?

The answer is simple but not easy: you learn to let go. You realise that your child is stronger than you think, that they'll survive the ups and downs, just like you did. You trust that the lessons you've taught them are about kindness, resilience, and self-worth. These lessons you teach will guide them when you can't be there to hold their hand.

And most importantly, you accept that motherhood is a journey of contradictions. It's about loving fiercely and letting go. It's about guiding and stepping back. It's about protecting and trusting that they'll find their own way, even when the world loses its balance.

Because at the end of the day, the paradox of motherhood is what makes it so beautifully messy, so heartbreakingly joyful, and so absolutely worth it.

Chapter 8

The Aftermath of Loss.

Life After the Last Goodbye.

In my first book, I poured my heart into capturing the raw, immediate sting of loss. I thought that writing about it would somehow free me from its grasp, as though putting the pain into words could somehow help me deal with the pain. But here's the hard truth about loss - it's relentless. It lingers like a shadow, always hovering just out of sight but never truly gone. You never get over it - you just learn to live around it. So here I am again, revisiting this familiar yet unwelcome subject, but this time from a different angle. The aftermath. It's not about the moment of loss itself but the slow, uninvited settling of its aftermath. How you navigate the quiet spaces it leaves behind, and how life moves forward even when you're not ready. The aftermath is its own beast, a quieter yet persistent ache that shapes who we become in its wake.

The hours after my dad passed remain etched into my soul like shadows that refuse to fade. People came from all corners of the country; some flew in from across the world, all to pay their respects. It was 4 am when we arrived home from the hospital, and it seemed like an entire entourage followed us home. Everyone was upset and completely shocked by the news of his sudden demise. As I gazed around my parent's home, I felt numb. I couldn't believe this was happening. I looked to my mother, hoping for some sign that she knew what was happening and had control over things, including the 'what now?'. But it was obvious she didn't. She was shattered, her face drained of all life, tears rolling down her face as if a running tap was left open. I swear it was like her body and mind hadn't quite caught up to one another. In retrospect, I think we were all in survival mode. At that moment, I realised that I had to step up. My grief had to take a back seat. I needed to be strong. For her. For us. For all the pieces of life that were left.

Nothing in my life ever broke me quite like watching him take his last breath, and nothing ever prepared me for how, in the aftermath of loss, people reveal their truest selves. You think it may be obvious that the people in your life are expected to care for you, right? Think again. True colours are a real thing, and sadly, they become apparent when faced with difficulty. It's the true friends and true family that stick around and support you when you need it most. In other instances, it was apparent that people who once seemed vibrant and cheerful in my dad's presence became distant, their warmth replaced by a cold, unfamiliar indifference. The same voices that echoed "family first" sentiments and promises of unwavering support vanished into whispers of emptiness. Grief, I learned, is an isolating force. It weighs you down, rendering you heavy and too burdensome for others to carry. It swallows you whole, and in doing so, it makes you feel invisible.

Within a few hours, I was thrust into a whirlwind of the mechanical tasks that follow death - legalities, paperwork, the 'admin' of loss. But no one warns you how suffocating it feels to sort through the remnants of someone's life while barely holding your own together. I had to push aside my pain and compartmentalise my heartache, as though grief was something that could be paused, tucked away for later.

As I walk down the hallway of my mom's home toward his office. His space. The place where his presence had always lingered, steady and comforting. And as I stepped inside, I could almost feel him there with me, like a shadow hovering just out of reach. He was guiding me with that quiet strength as he always had. His presence was tangible, so real that I could almost feel him standing behind me, pointing me toward the path I wasn't ready to walk alone. And yet, somehow, I wasn't walking alone. Every step was a painful stroll through memories - his laughter, his scent, the way he'd call me into his office just to talk. And there I was, moving forward, without him, facing the impossible task of navigating life without the man who had always shown me the way.

I discovered my safe spaces in the most unexpected moments, under the steady stream of the shower and in the loud hum of the hair dryer. It was the sound, the sheer constancy of the water cascading over me, and the warm, rhythmic whirring of the dryer that gave me a strange kind of permission to let go. In those moments, when the world outside fell away, I could finally fall apart. The water masked my sobs, blending with the tears that came in waves, and the white noise of the dryer drowned out my cries and the chaos in my mind. These were the only places where I felt the weight of my grief could be released, where I could cry with wild abandon without fear of judgment or concern for anyone else. For months, these rituals became my refuge. These were spaces where my heartbreak was no longer hidden but allowed to be felt in its rawest form. The shower and the hair dryer became my sanctuary, places where I was allowed to break, piece by piece, in the hope that maybe one day, I would feel ok again.

When you go through pain like this, you realise that simply having days that feel 'okay' becomes sufficient. The need to chase after 'amazing' fades, and you're grateful for the simple moments of just being, where life is steady and calm, and that's all you truly need. Not hurt. Not broken and Not lost. Just ok is good enough.

Loss can only be experienced. It cannot be explained. A few of my close friends have lost their dads over the recent years as well, and they will attest to this. I always say if you have lost, it's like you are in a club. A depressing club of people who know what you are feeling. But it is a comforting club because of people who know what you are feeling.
So, if you happen to experience loss, I really hope you find your tribe to support you. They don't even need to say anything. They just need to be there knowing what you are going through.

Lately, I've been dreaming of my deceased relatives, as if they come to visit me from a different realm. Last night, I dreamt of my grandmother trying on a beautiful dress, preparing to go somewhere I couldn't follow. And maybe it's because this weekend marks ten years since my dad died. Ten years. A decade feels like a lifetime and like a moment all at once. The dream brought a strange comfort, and I thought maybe as a form of therapy, I should write a letter to my dad. Say what I want to say, then remove it from existence.

So I sat at my desk, opened my laptop, and started typing.

"Dear Dad,

I miss you - more than I could ever put into words. I miss your laugh. I miss your jokes. I miss your big bear hugs. Nothing can compare. There was still so much I needed to learn from you. I wasn't done. I wasn't ready to say goodbye. I guess that's part of the difficulty, dealing with the fact that I never got to say goodbye. My last words will forever taunt me. "I'll see you in 30 minutes, Dad". The time never came. I wonder what it was like for you in theatre before they put you under. Did they tell you how severe it was? How risky it would be? Did they tell you they called us? Did they tell you what we said?

We weren't ready, Dad.

There's so much to say. I can't explain the void you left in our lives. The hole in our hearts has never been filled. It's been 10 years, and whilst it does feel like a lifetime without you, it also feels like we just watched you take your last breath. I can still feel that heartbreak. That intense pain when you left.

I wish we could visit you. I wish we had the chance to say goodbye. God, I wish I could introduce you to your grandchildren. I wish I could phone you whenever I need to, whenever I want to.

I got that promotion, Dad. I bought that house and then another one. I traveled, and I had another kid. She's just like you, too. She's funny and loving, always pulling pranks, and is hilarious. It's like having a piece of you with me. All the grandkids talk about their 'Grandpa' as if they know you. Just as you did when you were with us, making everyone a friend. You have 4 incredible little friends here in your grandkids, and they absolutely adore you. I like to think that you met them before we did.

Mom is ok; she's different now. Her light hasn't been the same. She has such a void in her life. So much of her was wrapped up in you. So much of her went with you. But it's ok, we're watching over her. Even though sometimes she thinks we are acting like 'the parent'.

Dad, I know you're my guardian angel, always by my side, and I feel your presence every day. If heaven had visiting hours, I would be there in a heartbeat, asking the angels if I could take you back home with me. But I know what they'd say - they'd remind me that this is how it's meant to be and reassure me that your love is still with me, always. Still, I can't help but wish it were different. But for now, I carry you with me in every step I take, knowing that while we may be apart, a part of you lives on in me, guiding me until we meet again.

Love has no bounds. I will love you forever.
Love,
Ally (aka Baby Joe)

PS: I will forever blame that bastard, Dr Bee, for taking chances with your life. I hope you lightening bolt his ass.

There are days when I still expect the phone to ring, when I half-think it's him on the other end, ready with some fatherly wisdom to steer me through whatever mess life throws my way. And I know that day will never come again. Losing someone close to you changes your view on life in ways that are both profound and irreversible. Suddenly, the things that once seemed so important, career ambitions, trivial arguments, the rush of everyday obligations- shrink in the shadow of your grief. You become acutely aware of how fragile everything is, how fleeting time truly is, and how precious even the smallest moments are. Life, once filled with certainty, becomes a series of questions - about purpose, meaning, and how to move forward when a piece of your heart is missing. You start to see the world differently, realising that nothing is promised and that love, connection, and the people you hold dear are the only constants worth holding onto. Grief strips away the noise, forcing you to live with greater intention, cherish the quiet moments, and embrace the beauty of simply being present in a world that is forever changed.

As the days turn into weeks and the rawness of the loss begins to soften, you start to realise that grief isn't something you overcome. It's simply something you learn to live with. It becomes a part of your life, a quiet presence that walks beside you. But along with it, there's a deep sense of love that never fades. I truly believe that the people we lose never truly leave us. They're in the memories we cherish, the lessons they taught us, and the moments we carry forward in their honour. And though the weight of their absence remains, there's comfort in knowing that love is eternal, and in the quiet spaces of our hearts, they are always with us.

*If you haven't lost someone close to you, I encourage you to get your ducks in a row. I encourage you to educate yourself on the 'admin' of life - as depressing as that sounds. It's important.

Chapter 9

Halloween

The scary truth behind the mask

Halloween - A time when you're expected to juggle costume creation, candy procurement, and the fine art of dealing with the terrifying show of your kids sugar-induced hyperactivity. It all begins with the annual costume debate. Your 10-year-old is now at the age where their costume needs to be "epic" and "socially acceptable" in the world of prep school peer pressure. They've moved past the days of adorable pumpkins and pirates. This year, they want to be something "cool," like Taylor Swift or an intricate character from their favourite video game. Meanwhile, your 6-year-old is still in the 'cute' phase of costume selection. They're adamant about being a unicorn, complete with sparkles and a horn that might double as a hazard if they're not careful. Your attempts to find a unicorn costume that doesn't look like it's made of leftover tinsel and sheer desperation lead you to a series of late-night craft sessions, hot glue gun burns, and a lot of glitter - glitter that will inevitably end up in your house's nooks and crannies until next Halloween.

I'd say the buzz starts in September, to be fair. Kids' party invites are going out weeks in advance, which automatically opens up the conversation around what the plans are for Halloween. Plans, meaning, what's mom got to do to ensure that it is a spooktacular memory that gets embedded into your kid's life experience. Isn't that always the case? How we constantly push ourselves to be the best mom and give our kids the best childhood so they grow up to be the best versions of themselves.

This, however, does not come as a simple Uber delivery of candy and chucking on a witch's hat. The checklist already starts twirling in our minds, and it looks something like this:

1. Costume Decision: Will your kid's costume arrive by October 31st? (God hoping it fits)

2. Candy Stockpile: Buy "extra extra" candy for an unknown number of trick-or-treaters.

3. Pumpkin Carving: Find pumpkins. Also, I question if it's still a thing.

4. Costume Repairs: Have safety pins and tape ready for the inevitable costume malfunction.

5. Weather Watch: Check the forecast for rain, and prepare for the battle of "But you have to wear a jacket over that!"

6. Candy Quality Control: Sample a few pieces to make sure the candy is safe and honestly up to standard (because, let me tell you, the standards are high these days).

Nothing out of the ordinary and definitely nothing over the top. This is just the basic list that fell out of me. Why? Because I've been there, done that. I've learned from not having enough candy to not having safety pins on hand.

I can't help but wonder how these lists have evolved over the years and at what point things really start taking a turn for the OTT. In the 90's, you could grab an old bedsheet, cut some eye holes, and boom, you're a ghost. Nowadays, however, costumes are full-on productions, complete with LED lights, 3D-printed accessories, and makeup tutorials that would make a Hollywood makeup artist proud. Back then, you got a hodgepodge of sweets, including some questionable 'treats' like raisins, oranges, or those weird green and black-wrapped candies that no one ever liked. Nowadays, it's all about full-sized candy bars, organic options, and allergy-friendly treats.

But what really strikes me is how, despite the elaborate costumes, lights, and social media-ready moments, the biggest costume of all might be the one we wear every day. That's right, folks, I am spinning the 'trick or treat' into 'the masks we wear to feel complete'. This in itself has become somewhat of a talent of mine since becoming a mom. The ability to change a topic as smoothly as a silk pillowcase.

Case in point.

"You really want that piece of candy, hey? Let me tell you about how Santa and his elves make their own magical treats and TOYS! Gosh, How exciting!

Christmas is just over 100 days away. What do you think we should get for Grandma this year? Remember that trip we took with Grandma on the Safari? Gosh, those elephant babies were the cutest, weren't they? Dont you have a cute baby elephant stuffy? Let's go look for it."

Like I said. Smooth.

So, back to the masks we wear to feel complete. The thing is, it's not only on Halloween that we put on a mask; our modern lives are so curated and meticulously crafted that we're often playing a part. There's pressure to show up not just as yourself but as the best, most 'Instagrammable' version of yourself. The simplicity of showing up as a bedsheet ghost? That's long gone. Now, we layer on filters and masks not just for a night but for a lifestyle.

It's no wonder we have such high-functioning kids and are inevitably growing earlier than our parents. We're performing on Halloween level every other day. The bottom line is that life used to be simple, and the reality is that life will not pass as 'enough' in today's day and age. The masks have become part of the everyday costume. Oscar Wilde once said, "A mask tells us more than a face." This quote seems somehow intuitive based on the complexities of human nature and, fundamentally, our self-perception and identity. On the surface, a face is often seen as a direct reflection of who we are, our emotions, our thoughts, and our character. However, Wilde suggests that it is when we wear a mask and hide behind a facade that our true selves are most revealing. The reality is that a mask offers a sense of anonymity and freedom. We possibly feel liberated to a certain degree from the expectations and judgments of our surroundings, perhaps allowing us to express parts of ourselves that we usually keep hidden.

Take, for instance, a masquerade; people may behave more boldly or express emotions they normally suppress because the mask provides a layer of protection. This behaviour shows that sometimes, it is only when we are freed from the scrutiny of others that we allow our truest selves to emerge.

The idea is that what we present to the world daily - our "face" - is often a mask in itself. We carefully craft our public personas, hiding insecurities or socially unacceptable thoughts. The face we show might be more about conforming to societal norms than about revealing who we genuinely are. Conversely, when someone puts on an actual mask, they might reveal more of their authentic self than they do without it. The fact is, that we need to consider that the layers of identity we craft and the personas we present might conceal more than they reveal, and it is in the act of hiding that we often show the most.

●●●

As I was enjoying my morning chat with my sister-in-law, who, by the way, is one of those rare human beings who completely obliterates the stereotype of the 'difficult in-law.' Seriously, she's one of the most wonderful people on this planet. Oh, and did I mention she's a psychiatrist? Which is incredibly convenient for someone like me who's teetering on the edge of a midlife crisis most of the time. Anyway, we got to talking about her latest conference, and in typical fashion, she dropped one of those profound nuggets of wisdom that I instantly knew had to make its way into this book.

"So here's the thing," she began, launching into this insightful explanation about women entering their 40s. It turns out that as we tiptoe into our perimenopausal years, our oestrogen levels start to play a disappearing act. And here's the kicker: for those of us who've unknowingly struggled with mental health issues but have managed to keep it together thanks to our hormonal safety net, the decline in oestrogen can basically pull the rug out from under us. It's like our mental health issues have been wearing an invisibility cloak, and when the oestrogen levels dip - surprise! They're suddenly front and centre unmasked and demanding attention. I sat there, completely absorbed by how simply she explained something that affects so many of us, yet so few of us really talk about it.

She paused for dramatic effect (as psychiatrists tend to do), then leaned in and said something that stuck with me: "It all works... until it doesn't." I mean, isn't that just the most accurate description of midlife, womanhood, and, let's face it, life in general? We women are juggling so much all the time, often without a second thought to our mental health because, well, life doesn't stop for a check-in. But when things stop working, when our bodies and minds start to demand attention, we've been denying them, and it hits hard. So, I'm offering you this little gem in the hope it becomes your mantra, too. It's simple but profound: "It all works until it doesn't." And when it doesn't? That's when we really need to start paying attention. And most importantly - again - know you are not alone.

It is a slight detour from the lightheartedness of Halloween, but it is still relevant in terms of being true to yourself.

So there you have it, Halloween, the one day where the masks we wear are celebrated, and the chaos of parenting gets a sugar-coated twist. But here's the spooky truth: the masks we wear aren't just for October 31st. We've been wearing them all along, juggling life with a costume of 'I've got it all together.' The trick is in knowing when it's okay to take it off. Because, as my sister-in-law says, 'It all works... until it doesn't.' And when it doesn't, well, it's time to treat yourself to a little honesty and some full-sized candy bars. You've earned it!

Chapter 10

Finding family

The Ancestry Roulette

It all began with the passing of Queen Elizabeth. Suddenly, I found myself yearning to trace a royal lineage back to my own roots. Why not? After all, unless you're the eldest, even a king's descendants eventually fade into the ordinary. Take the British monarchy, for instance: If Elizabeth's less-famous sister, Margaret, had three kids, the first would be her heir. But once that child has their own children, those grandkids take precedence over Margaret's second and third children. And so it goes, generation after generation. That's just Margaret's line; imagine the tangled branches of Elizabeth's father's siblings and their siblings! What became of those forgotten royals?

In today's digital age, it's much easier to maintain a semblance of royalty through documented lineage. But back then, who knows how many noble bloodlines quietly slipped into obscurity? Anyway, all this royal rumination sparked a keen interest in uncovering my own heritage. So, I signed up for ancestry.com. There's something about clicking "submit" on your DNA sample that feels a bit like playing a biological game of roulette. You think you know what's going to come up: a sprinkle of Irish, a dash of French, maybe some Viking warrior genes that explain why you're not afraid of assembling furniture.

So I spit into the little vial, mailed it off, and waited for my results like a kid waiting for Santa.

Life carried on, with me pretty much forgetting about my lineage fixation. Waking up on a Saturday morning, which was surprisingly free of kids' parties and sports. The only thing I wanted to do was have a pyjama day, which in my world meant - no bra day. As I sit down on my favourite chair with my morning coffee, I habitually check my phone for updates and emails. There it was - my results from the DNA testing had arrived. With excitement, I opened it with the casual expectation of learning something like, "You're 27% British" or "Congratulations, you're related to someone who once owned a goat farm in Norway." I started navigating my way around the report. There were a few different tabs, and all seemed to offer various types of summaries and readings. It was a lot to consume, but I started with the first tab, which read "your heritage."
Another tab read "your connections," which sounded like just other people I may know who have signed up or one of those 'shares if you care' kind of algorithms. Clicking over, it says I've got 1016 connections, of which 1014 shared 1% or less of a DNA match. There was someone I shared an 11% DNA match with, which was my first cousin in New York. He and I have always been close, so it was nice to see him deemed genetically close, too.

Then, as I scrolled down, I saw there was someone I shared a 39% DNA match with. The only difference was I had never heard of this person before.

Ricaro from Italy. Still unsure of what information I was reading, I clicked on his name and noticed he didn't have a profile picture and not much information on his profile page. But two things were for certain, according to ancestry.com
1. He was a VERY close relative
2. I was no 'friend' of a Ricaro from Italy

I stared blankly at the screen, wondering what I had just uncovered.

I had questions. A lot of questions.

My mind subsequently began racing. Did my parents have some wild secret life? Maybe it's a dramatic fling they never mentioned over Sunday roast? Or was this some kind of epic clerical error, like the time my order of socks from Amazon somehow turned into a hair curler? But there was that little tickle of excitement, too. Could it be? Could I have another family member, someone who maybe shares my quirky sense of humour or unfortunate unibrow?

I messaged, let's call him "Potential Relative", and in my typical overthinking fashion, the message took forever to write. I mean, how do you start that conversation? "Hi there, you don't know me, but apparently, we might share some DNA?" Not exactly your standard icebreaker.

I was certain that, in true comedic fashion, this wasn't going to be a neatly wrapped-up Hallmark moment. Oh no. I found myself beginning to spiral into a mini-identity crisis mentally. Am I made up of who I think I'm made up of? What if I'm the missing link to his family network? Wait, I know Dad studied in Italy. So perhaps he's the culprit. Wait again, Do I have to explain this whole saga to my family, and they react like I've brought home a stray puppy without asking permission? Do I now have to awkwardly introduce him at family dinners like, "Hey, everyone, meet your surprise relative?"

At one point, I even imagined throwing a family reunion where everyone's name tag reads "Maybe Related?" because at this point, who really knows?

I stopped right there.

Within 5 minutes of me driving myself partly crazy, I received a notification that there was 1 unread message in my inbox. It was from Ricaro. When he replied, it was both the weirdest and most exhilarating exchange of my life.

"Hi, Ally,
I've been waiting for this day for so long. The day when I received an email confirming I ' have a DNA match.' Today is that day.
I don't know where to start, but I hope you are sitting down.
My name is Ricaro; I'm 49 years old. I was adopted when I was 4 months old from a children's home in Florence, Italy. I've spent most of my adult life wondering if I would ever find ... well .. I guess my biological family. I was born at a time when records of illegitimate babies weren't kept very well. It took me a lot of digging to find a basic story of how I came about. All I know is that I was born to a single young woman. Her family disapproved of her

keeping a child without being married. So I believe they kept her hidden until I was born, then put me in a children's home and left. I've been trying to track down my roots, and until today, I've not had much luck. I believe we may be half-siblings, depending on the probability of this platform being used. Could we chat further, please?"

My heart sank. Siblings!!!
This wasn't just some clerical error. This man had been searching for his roots, and apparently, I was part of his story.

I shouted for Roux to come quickly, and immediately, my watch started vibrating with the screen flashing back at me, "Abnormal heart rate detected." As I read and reread this message from "Potential Relative", I wanted to jump on a plane and see this person face to face, but I also so desperately wished my dad was still alive so I could unravel this mystery.

I responded

"Hi Ricaro, wow! That's a lot to digest, if I'm being honest. I would definitely want to chat further. Are you open to a telephone call or video call at all? I know it's A LOT to ask and A LOT to take in. But if you are, I think I have the courage to do so. Hopefully, we can chat soon, Ally"

He responded Immediately

"Hi, Ally,
Thank you so much for your quick response. I know this is overwhelming, and I can't even begin to imagine what must be going through your mind

right now. Honestly, I feel the same way. It's surreal, like something out of a movie, and yet, here we are, facing this unexpected connection.

I'm definitely open to a phone or video call. I think it would help make this all feel a bit more real. It's a lot, yes, but I'm ready if you are.

Whenever you feel comfortable, just let me know a time that works for you. I understand if you need a little more time to process everything, too. Either way, I'm here, and I'm really looking forward to chatting.

Talk soon,

Ricaro"

After taking a moment to breathe and try to control my anxiety, I decided to send off my number and say I'd be waiting for the video call. I assured him that I was free at that moment and was able to take the call.

Within 3 minutes, my phone rang. It was a video call.

I clicked 'Answer'.

The face staring back at me was miraculous. We both laughed, and in between the laughter, we said words like "Hi" and "Oh my god." Ricaro looked like a younger, slightly different, but very similar version of my dad. It's strange to go back to that moment mentally, but I remember thinking, "we have the same eyes."

After a few seconds or minutes of staring, laughing, and getting out minimal words, we finally started chatting. He told me his life story, and I told him mine. We talked for hours, comparing notes, sharing baby photos with each other, and uncovering the undeniable truth: we were half-siblings. The resemblance was one aspect of this surety, but more so, there was an incredible connection that I felt instantly with this person I'd never heard of before in my life.

Beyond the initial shock, there was something oddly comforting about the whole situation. The idea is that even when we think we've figured out who we are and where we come from, life can still throw these little plot twists our way. In retrospect, I can acknowledge that there is also a strange kind of beauty in finding family in unexpected places. We spend so much of our lives defining ourselves by our immediate connections: mom, dad, siblings, and cousins. Suddenly, you're confronted with the possibility that the definition of "family" is bigger, broader, and way messier than you ever imagined. And that's kind of cool. Scary but cool.

So, what happens next? Well, Potential Brother and I are navigating this brave new world of siblinghood, cautiously optimistic and laughing at how ridiculous and wonderful it is that in the vastness of the internet and the world, we somehow managed to find each other through a test designed to tell me I'm 2% Swedish. Who knew it would lead to this?

When I said these words to Ricaro, he then said, "But you know there's the disclaimer, right?"

Sure, this is the face of someone in the know. I just click, click, click away and hardly ever read the fine print.

Apparently, the disclaimer was in a big yellow box that we had to accept as legal protection for <u>ancestry.com</u> not to get sued for revealing life-altering information. "For example," he said, "Like finding siblings".

We laughed. I was glad he got my vibe, and I definitely got his.

Maybe this is the start of a beautiful sibling relationship. Or maybe it'll just make for the best "Guess what happened to me?" story at every future dinner party. Either way, it's a win in my book. Pun intended.

As the call ended, I sat in stunned silence, my mind racing. I was trying to process the fact that I had a half-brother living in Italy. It wasn't just a wild piece of trivia anymore; it was my reality. How do you even begin to explain something like this to your family? "Oh, by the way, I found out we have a sibling, and he's from Florence." Casual. My husband, Roux, was still trying to wrap his head around it, too. He sat across from me, sipping his coffee as if we hadn't just dropped a bombshell into our lives. Addison, our younger daughter, blissfully unaware, was dancing around the living room in her princess dress, completely oblivious to the fact that her family tree had just gained a new branch.

Roux, ever the calm and collected one, finally broke the silence. "Well, this is… a lot." Yah, that's the understatement of the century. But what could we do? I couldn't go back in time and know what I'd just discovered. There was no "undo" button for this kind of revelation. We were in uncharted territory, and there was no guidebook on how to navigate the surprise sibling scenario. All I knew was that I had to tell my mom, and soon.

That conversation, though, was going to be tricky. I imagined sitting my mom and siblings down, starting with something simple like, "So, funny story..." But nothing about this was funny, at least not in the traditional sense. I knew my mom would probably cry. Not in a sad way, but in that overwhelmed, emotional way that moms tend to do when things get too big to process. My dad? Well, if he was around, he'd probably crack some weird joke about getting around in his younger days, but I'm sure I'd see the uncertainty in his eyes. He'd wonder what he missed, who he might've hurt. He was a gentle giant with a heart of gold. The guilt would have crept in, and for instance, I was kind of glad he wasn't around to feel any guilt and pain in this regard.

But beyond the awkward conversations and the emotional rollercoaster, there was a part of me that was excited. I had another sibling - an actual older sibling! Growing up as the eldest child, I'd always dreamed of what it would be like to have a big brother or sister. I'd imagined the camaraderie, the fights, the shared history. And now, after all these years, here he was - Ricaro, my half-brother from halfway around the world.

The question was, what came next? It wasn't like we could just slot Ricaro into our lives as if he'd always been there. We were separated by more than just distance. There were entire lifetimes we didn't share - birthdays, holidays, milestones. We hadn't grown up with the same stories, the same parents. Yet, despite all that, I felt this strange sense of connection, like he was meant to find me, and I was meant to find him. I couldn't help but feel my dad's presence in this surreal discovery. He had some angelic powers that made me question my ancestry when the Queen died. Like he had some finger in the pie of bringing Ricaro and me together, it's a miraculous thought - and I believe it wholeheartedly.

As I sat there, the possibilities unfolded in front of me. Maybe one day, we'd all meet in person. I could already picture it: us visiting Florence, Abby, and Addison, running through cobblestone streets, their little voices echoing in the alleys as they chased after her newly discovered uncle. Or maybe Ricaro would come here, standing awkwardly in my kitchen as we made small talk over tea and tried to catch up on a lifetime of missed moments.

The reality was that this was a new chapter in all of our lives, and while it was full of unknowns, it was also full of potential. I didn't know where this journey with Ricaro would take us, but I knew one thing for sure: family isn't just about who's been there all along, 'cause let's face it. Those who have been there all along tend to be real let-downs when times get tough. This entire experience showed me that it's also about the surprises that come along when you least expect them. Whether we share parents or just a piece of DNA, I've found a new connection in the most unexpected way. And in this crazy, unpredictable life, that feels like a pretty great twist. It might not be the fairytale I originally set out to uncover, but it's my story. And in the grand, messy, unpredictable tale of life, that's more than enough.

Chapter 11

Self-Care Shenanigans

Zen Mode Activated..... Until Someone Asks for a Snack

Let's get one thing straight: bodies change. It's a fact of life, as inevitable as taxes, wrinkles, and the sudden urge to nap after a big meal. But here's the thing - why is it that society keeps telling us to fight those changes like we're going to win some battle against time? Reality check? Time always wins. But here's another truth - time has a way of making us wiser, funnier, and, dare I say, even more fabulous.

Let's face it: the late 30s can be a whirlwind of responsibilities and expectations. Whether you're balancing a demanding job, managing family dynamics, or simply trying to juggle a social life with personal goals, it's easy to push self-care to the back burner. But this chapter is about reclaiming your right to prioritise yourself amid the chaos.

Welcome to the reality of body positivity as you approach 40, where it's less about the size of your jeans and more about the size of your confidence. If your 20s were all about trying to squeeze into those skinny jeans and your 30s were about realising they were just never going to happen again, your 40s are the era of embracing the stretch, the curves, and yes, even a slight jiggle.

Let's talk about the shifting relationship with your body.

So, your body isn't exactly the same as it was at 25. But guess what? Neither are you, and that's a good thing. The body you're rocking now has been through some stuff, some serious stuff that's made you stronger, smarter, and, yes, maybe a little softer around the edges. And let's be honest, isn't it time we stop measuring our worth by the firmness of our thighs and start celebrating the fact that we've got thighs that can still carry us through a busy day?

This is where the magic of self-care comes in. And no, I'm not talking about slapping on a sheet mask and calling it a day (though if that's your thing, you do, you boo). I'm talking about self-care, that's about nurturing your body and soul in ways that make you feel good - not because you're chasing some impossible standard, but because you deserve to feel fabulous in your own skin.

As we enter the grand finale of our 30s, where our body has decided to embark on its own unique journey. Its time to forget about the thigh gap; let's talk about the mind gap - the space where youthful insecurities once lived, now replaced by the wisdom of embracing your fabulous, evolving self.

So, let's address the elephant in the room: your body is going to change. It's going to shift and occasionally surprise you with new quirks. Remember when your metabolism was like a well-oiled machine? Recently, I've been told it's now more like an old car that sometimes needs a push to get going. Thanks, Jenna-Lee! But here's the secret - it's all part of the grand, messy, and sometimes hard-to-accept adventure of aging.

So before our bodies embrace a 'vintage' status, let's use this time to up our TLC and have no scrubs because all you need is love from you. 90's kids will get this reference quicker than most.

Here's where I think the shift needs to be made: we need to be able to embrace our bodies with the same enthusiasm we once reserved for new fashion trends. Think of it as an opportunity to build a new wardrobe, one that's not just about hiding but rather about celebrating. It's more about prioritising our well-being over appearance. It's time to embrace and practice the two words that are surely beginning to flood your feeds: Self-Care.

In your late 30s, self-care isn't about grand gestures; it's about the small, meaningful practices that nurture your body, mind, and soul. We need to consider self-care as a daily ritual, a series of moments dedicated to honouring who we are and what we need. It starts with acknowledging that we deserve to feel good, both physically and emotionally. This might mean carving out time for activities that bring us joy, embracing rest without guilt, and probably something as simple as being present in the moment. Enjoy that quiet cup of coffee at 6 am before everyone wakes up. Take that walk around the block if the time presents itself. Read a few pages of a book that's caught your attention - even if it is the latest gossip column. Remember that these moments are not luxuries, but they are necessities. We need them to keep ourselves grounded and, quite frankly, sane.

I guess this is an opportunity and time where we get to re-introduce ourselves to our bodies. We get to apply some EQ and be more empathetic to ourselves.

The hardest part?

Accepting this truth.

• • •

There I was, a busy 37-year-old me, in the midst of knowing it all, including all about self-care, with not an ounce of practice of what I preach. I've got my yoga mat collecting dust in a corner, meditation apps taking up space on my phone, and a poor skincare regime that involves splashing water on my face and hoping for the best. My schedule, though, is another ball game. Full of work, social obligations, family gatherings, and an insanely unhealthy addiction to caffeine.

I was pretty much always saying I'd 'take a break' as soon as I'd done 'just this one more thing'. Expect that 'one more thing' became 'many more things.' I was at a point of accepting my daily balanced meal containing coffee for breakfast, popcorn for lunch, chocolate, chips, and the occasional protein bar in between, and, of course, some processed chicken et al. for dinner. I honestly thought I was on a roll! In my prime. Winging it. Doing what needed to be done. I was all these wonderful things. So, what could possibly go wrong?

Well, it turns out a lot.

One fateful Tuesday, I found myself at the office, knee-deep in a deadline and running purely on espresso fumes. I hadn't eaten anything but a questionable granola bar, and I'd been hunched over my computer for so long that my spine began resembling a question mark. My late dad would shout "Back straight, chest out, stomach in!" - I needed him back in my life so much. I was totally ignoring the subtle warning signs (like, oh, I don't know, the throbbing headache, the dizziness, and the fact that my left eye had been twitching for three days); I just powered through. After all, this is what I do.

The truth is, my body was in a "Fuck you" kinda mood, and by mid-afternoon, it decided it was over me and my bull shit.

One moment, I was typing furiously, and the next, I was sprawled out on the office floor, a human pretzel, if you may, full of dehydration and stress, and completely neglected any sense of self-care. My colleagues panicked, and an ambulance was called. I've always been full of the drama. But this time, it had become an emergency situation.

Cut to the hospital, where I groggily awoke to the wind gushing at my face as they pushed my bed down the corridor. They pulled me into my bed bay and checked all my vitals. A doctor soon approached and had a slight but clear shake of his head. He was either not impressed or knew my dramatic tendencies all too well. The latter could not have been true, as I was sure this was our first meeting.

"Ally," he began, with the tone of someone who's about to deliver some tough love, "when was the last time you had a proper meal?"

I blinked, trying to remember. "Umm...Does coffee count?"

The doctor didn't even crack a smile. "No. And when was the last time you slept for more than five hours?"

I recall scratching my head like a cartoon character does when they are trying to recall a situation. "Uh... there was that one Saturday recently?"

The doctor sighed. "You've completely burned yourself out. You're dehydrated, sleep-deprived, malnourished, and your body basically gave you a time-out."

As I lay there, hooked up to an IV drip like I was at some kind of day spa treatment, I realised just how absurd this whole situation was. I hadn't practiced self-care in what felt like ever, and now here I was, getting a crash course in "what not to do." I couldn't shake my own head at the ridiculousness of it all.

The doctor gave me a list of instructions that read like a manual for being a functioning human: eat regular meals, drink water, sleep for more than five hours a night, and maybe try yoga (my mind shouting 'for real this time'). As

I nodded along, secretly wondering if "self-care" was just code for "adulting properly." Either way, I knew I was going to have to make some changes.

As I left the hospital, with my IV drip replaced by a giant bottle of water, I mentally made a promise to myself: Ally, you need actually to start taking care of yourself from now on. And by "take care," this time, I really mean more than just a fleeting attempt at taking care of yourself once a month and calling it a day.

• • •

As you journey through your late 30s, the notion of self-care transforms from a trendy catchphrase into a necessity. Gone are the days when this notion might have meant a sporadic spa day or a passing indulgence in a bubble bath. Now, it's a fundamental practice that's not so much about occasional treats but more about a daily commitment to your well-being - to your mind, body, and soul. We need to acknowledge and remember that this 'self-care' space is not an indulgence. It's a fundamental need.

As you step into this new chapter of your life, remember this - your body is your lifelong companion, not your adversary. Treat it with kindness, love it for the incredible things it does, and embrace the changes with a sense of humour and joy. After all, if you're going to age, you might as well do it with style, body positivity, and a hearty laugh because every wrinkle tells a tale.

It is not quite a tale as old as time, but it is definitely a tale of beauty and the beyond. For those of us who've spent decades scrutinising every fine line and obsessing over every wrinkle, we are about to experience a shift, and it will be like stepping into a whole new world. One where perfection is overrated, and authenticity is the real showstopper. And to reference Disney one more time, 'live happily ever after'.

The quest for flawlessness and glass skin is exhausting. We've spent years trying to meet impossible standards set by our younger selves, society, and a whole host of airbrushed celebrities. But here's the thing: Beauty is no longer about looking like a photoshopped version of yourself. It's about owning every part of who you are, from the laugh lines that tell tales of joy to the stretch marks that whisper secrets of growth.

If there's one thing you need to do as you enter your 40s, it's to stop trying to be perfect. Seriously, perfection is so last decade. The new you is all about "im-perfection" - emphasis on the "im." Your flaws are what make you interesting. Let's think of it like every wrinkle is just a smile that never faded, and every grey hair is a strand of wisdom poking through. Let's face it: self-care is no longer a luxury; it's survival. And if my story of Espresso-fueled hospital visits hasn't scared you into prioritising yourself, then maybe this will: You deserve better. You deserve more than just 'surviving.' You deserve to wake up and actually have your body feel good. Not because it looks like a supermodel's, but because it's yours, and it's done some serious work to get you here. After all, perfection is overrated, but loving yourself? That's timeless.

Chapter 12

Family Holidays

The good. The bad and the Oh-Crap!

Down here in the Southern Hemisphere, year-end holidays are less about snowflakes and more about sunburns, with a generous helping of the usual suspects - family, too much pudding, drama, tinsel, and a side of chaos. Me, being somewhat of a self-designated family holiday planner. Which, in 2024, isn't exactly the same as it was when my mother held that title in the '90s. Back then, family holidays were a much simpler affair. Picture it: a family of four crammed into a car with a trunk packed tighter than a sardine can. We had a road atlas, a bag of snacks that miraculously lasted the entire trip, and a Walkman to drown out the occasional sibling squabble. Entertainment was provided by roadside attractions, "I Spy" games, and the endless anticipation of arriving at a destination that usually meant a modest hotel with a pool.

Fast forward to today, and family holidays have transformed into high-tech, luxury extravaganzas. Instead of a road atlas, we rely on GPS, an infallible guide that often leads us into the middle of nowhere while calmly suggesting we make a U-turn. Our snacks are now meticulously curated into organic, gluten-free, and artisanal varieties because heaven forbid we encounter a non-Keto-friendly treat. The kids, equipped with tablets and headphones, are entertained by streaming services that can instantly transport them to distant worlds without so much as a glance out the window.

Yet, despite the tech overload and luxury accommodations, there was still something undeniably special about those '90s road trips has been lost in translation. There was a certain magic in the way we once looked forward to each rest stop, how we spent hours marvelling at the "world's largest something or the other," and how every family photo was an honest snapshot of our unfiltered selves. Today's vacations, while more comfortable and connected, often come with the trade-off of curated experiences and planned itineraries, leaving little room for the spontaneous, messy moments that once made family holidays memorable.

●●●

As we drove up to the beach estate, my heart swelled with pride. I had meticulously planned this vacation to be the perfect family getaway. With 57 relatives in tow, cousins, aunts, uncles, and grandparents - I envisioned days drenched in sunshine, endless laughter, and perfectly captured memories for all. Naturally, to add to my already overflowing plate, I thought it to be a brilliant idea to organise a grand family photo shoot on the beach. After all, it's not very often that every member of this very large family gets together. And besides, who better to manage chaos than a seasoned juggler of family, work, and everything in between?

The car was jam-packed, the cooler was bursting with snacks, and my husband, bless his heart, was doing his best to look relaxed amid the highly organised chaos I had orchestrated. I was determined to make this holiday unforgettable. Our grand plan was not only to enjoy the sun, but I had become so fixated on immortalising the moment in a way that can only be done with professional photography. Everyone had signed up with enthusiasm, and I was thrilled! Not all buy-ins to my ideas are usually easily accepted, but this was a no-brainer even for the less enthused Fam Bam members.

As I rallied the troops for the photo shoot, the day seemed perfect. The sun was shining, the waves were rolling in, and everyone was in high spirits. I had meticulously planned out each pose and even brought a bag of props: a beach ball, a frisbee, and a whole bunch of cheesy "We Are Family" type signs.

"Mom, look at the sandcastle I built!" my eldest, Abby, proudly announced, her face smeared with sunblock and sand.

"That's amazing, sweetheart!" I replied, though my eyes were fixed on the list of things still to do. But, as any seasoned vacation organiser knows, things rarely go according to plan. The first hiccup appeared in the form of dark clouds creeping over the horizon. As I wrangled children into their groupings based on the shot list I had carefully created, the heavens decided to open up. "Just a passing shower," I assured everyone as we scrambled to cover our hair - god forbid the fizzy fairies make an appearance and grace us with not so graceful - oversized manes.

Then came the makeup catastrophe. My sister-in-law, determined to look "beach chic," applied her lipstick with the finesse of a Picasso painting. One glance at her face, and I knew our perfect family portrait would likely resemble something from a circus. No joke.

As if on cue, my nephew decided that the beach was the ideal place for a drop-and-spray situation, resulting in his mother having an utter canary and, in turn, with him then flinging sand and sobbing uncontrollably. Part of me thought, 'Poor little guy, just trying to do his business as nature intended.' The other part of me was like, 'Mate, for the love of all things sandy, get your pee-formance under control'. Uncle Joe was now four whiskeys down, questioning everyone's life choices - out loud.

As the photographer, the poor soul who had been promised a beach day but was now waist-deep in family drama struggled to get everyone into position; I was running around like a headless chicken - touching up makeup, adjusting outfits, and dealing with crying babies who have had another sandy dummy ripped away from them with the intent to rinse off.

"We just need to get everyone to smile!" I declared, attempting to guide a group of restless toddlers who appeared to be more interested in a sand fight than family unity. "Just a few more photos, everyone!"

The sun decided to make an appearance, but not before a sudden gust of wind, which turned Aunt Linda's hat into a sail, propelling it directly into Uncle Bobby's face. This resulted in a comical, if slightly embarrassing, series of photos that would later be known as "The Hat Incident of 2021."

Despite my best efforts, we seemed to be caught in a comedy of errors. The rain continued, and the once-perfect beach backdrop transformed into a muddy mess. The photographer was now playing referee between the kids and the adults, and the increasingly soggy clothes and beach hair, which was very far off from the wishful Farrah Fawcett flocks, we had intended.

After what felt like an eternity of trying to convince my tearful niece that the beach was a magical place and that the sharks could not get to her, I found myself sitting on a towel, drenched and defeated. My husband, sensing the breaking point, came over and wrapped an arm around me.

"Maybe we should just forget about the photos," he suggested gently.

But just then, a small voice tugged at my shirt. It was Addison, my baby, holding up a "We are Family Forever" sign, her eyes bright with hope.

"Mommy, we're having fun, right? That's what matters."

At that moment, I realised that while the perfect photoshoot had eluded us, we were making memories in our own imperfect way. Laughter had replaced the planned poses, and the chaos had become our unique brand of family fun.

As the rain tapered off and the sun made a valiant attempt at returning, we decided to improvise. We took our photos with wet hair, smudged makeup, and a lot of love. The kids ran around, splashing in the puddles, and the adults, despite the mishaps, managed to crack a few genuine smiles.

By the end of the day, I looked around at my family, soaked but happy, and knew that the holiday had been a success, not because of perfect photos or flawless planning, but because of the shared moments of joy, togetherness, and a funny story to look back on.

So, while the beach may not have given us a picture-perfect photo, it had given us something far better: a day filled with laughter, love, and the reminder that the best memories are often the ones we least expect.

● ● ●

Family holidays for me have become more about making memories and ensuring I create those threads of yarn that will ultimately be woven into the tapestry of my kids' childhood. I'm almost obsessed with ensuring they have opportunities and experiences that give them the best memories to look back on. So, while it all sounds picturesque and possibly OCD at a high level, the reality of family holidays is that it's a time when we all come together to eat food no one asked for, play games that incite arguments, and wear matching outfits that make us look like we're auditioning for a Hallmark special. For some, it's a truly magical time filled with love, laughter, and joy. For others, it's a prison sentence wrapped in tinsel and good intentions.

I am confidently one of the "THOSE" people. Yep, I'm the one most of you dread. I live for the excitement of it all and more often than not, I tend to generally go OTT (over the top). My blood runs purely on Christmas carols during December, and my social calendar is filled with mostly self-inflicted gatherings. I will happily wear reindeer antlers while sipping mulled wine at 10 a.m. and lead the charge in organising holiday-themed charades. Chances are, I've ordered personalised gifts for presents. So watch out if you want a padel bag from Santa. You're getting one with your name engraved on it!

But I get it; for some of you, this sounds like pure horror. Some of you are, let's say... a little more tepid in the festivity madness. So, to the Grinches of our gatherings, don't worry, I've seen it all (mostly from my family): the tactics, the excuses, the made-up illnesses - all to get you out of making memories and appeasing the enthusiastic organisers.

Believe it or not, I am here for you. I've put together a few tips on how to be more strategic in your approach to pooping the parties. Why, you ask?

Because of this overachieving, Virgo has had her fair share of obvious excuses, and frankly, I'd like to see you up your game. So here goes:

1. The Great Escape Plan

If you're dreading the holidays like a kid dreads broccoli, your first step is always to have an escape plan. Don't rely on faux "work emergencies," sudden allergies to pine trees, or the "I'm too sick" excuse. Hear me out... just. be. honest.

2. The Art of Stealth Napping

Why suffer through Aunt Linda's *"How-to-Make-a-Turkey-Selfie-on-Snapchat"* presentation when you can sneak away for a nap? Scout out the least trafficked room and slowly slip away right after the "What's new in your life?" interrogation, and emerge 30 minutes later, refreshed and blissfully unaware of the latest family gossip.

3. Mastering the Fake "Helpfulness" Move

If you want to avoid conversation, keep your hands busy. Washing dishes, chopping onions, or even aggressively reorganising the spice rack all grant you an air of busy importance. It also makes you immune to small talk because "Sorry, I just need to finish this 'garlic peeling' before I can chat!" Perfect.

4. The Food Coma Feint

Overeat strategically. Everyone knows post-dinner is the perfect time to slip into a blissful food coma that gives you a free pass on the "fun" family bonding activities. When you're asked to join in on a game, simply rub your stomach and murmur something about "digesting."

5. Distract with "Holiday Trivia"

When the dreaded political debates or probing personal questions inevitably arise, I recommend having some random holiday trivia up your sleeve. "Did you know that the largest gingerbread house ever built was over 2,500 square feet?" Boom - topic change. It's impossible to argue when everyone's Googling "world's largest gingerbread house."

In the end, it's not really about how much the family holiday traditions have evolved. From '90s road trips with car games and cassette tapes to today's over-the-top luxury vacations with GPS and gluten-free snacks. It's about finding the joy hidden within the chaos, embracing the unexpected, and realising that the imperfect moments are often the ones we'll remember (and laugh about) the most. Whether it's a sunburnt beach day, a failed family photo op, or a food coma-induced nap on the couch, the heart of family holidays remains the same: making memories and surviving the madness - together.

So, to my less-enthused comrades, know that you're not alone. Whether you're counting down the minutes until it's all over or fully immersing yourself in the festive fray, there's a survival strategy for everyone. You may be hiding under the mistletoe while I'm out there leading the charge in holiday karaoke, but just remember - you've got this. Who knows? You might even crack a smile or two along the way. After all, if you can endure family holidays, you can endure anything - including Aunt Lindas fruit cake.

Chapter 13

Change, Challenges, and Chuckles

The Secret Ingredients to Midlife Mischief!

It's all too easy to get swept up in the grandeur of the big picture, neglecting the small triumphs that truly shape our journey. Each step forward, no matter how modest, deserves its own celebration. I can advocate this philosophy with conviction, but living by it? That's another story entirely. The age-old adage proves itself once again: it's far easier said than done. I find myself constantly chasing a sense of accomplishment that always seems just out of reach. Perhaps it's because I place such immense pressure on myself always to do more and to be more. I second-guess my abilities, doubting whether I've done, well, enough even when there are clear reasons to be proud.

This self-doubt, I suspect, is deeply rooted in a fear of failure, one that has woven itself into the very fabric of my being. It's a fear that took hold during my schooling years, where the pursuit of 'being the best' was less a personal ambition and more a mandate driven by community standards and the expectation to display one's results in the local newspaper publicly. Back then, if your name didn't appear, you were labeled a failure. And if it did, anything less than a D for distinction was viewed as a public embarrassment, a scarlet letter of mediocrity. Not every family subscribed to this peculiar pressure, thankfully, but for many of us, it became a defining feature of our formative years.

The truth is, no matter where you are in the world, this pressure lingers. It takes on different forms, but if you're someone who strives to succeed, that weight follows you, casting its shadow over every achievement. And perhaps that's why, despite any accomplishments, I continue to doubt myself because of that deep-rooted fear of falling short, which was instilled so long ago and has never truly left.

From my various readings on the evolution of facing fears comes a large investment in embracing change. I can vaguely see that despite having a lifelong battle with the fear of failure, there's an undeniable truth that I've come to recognise, even if it took years of soul-searching to fully understand. Facing your fears head-on and learning to embrace change are not only liberating but can also open the door to something truly unexpected - fun.

It sounds almost counterintuitive, doesn't it? The idea is that confronting those deeply ingrained fears, the ones that keep you up at night and make you question your worth could lead to joy, laughter, and even a lightness in your soul. When we stop allowing fear to dictate every move we make, we create space for new experiences, space for spontaneity, and space for fun.

It's in those moments of vulnerability when we step out of the tightly controlled world we've built to protect ourselves that the most surprising things can happen. Embracing change, whether it's a career shift, a lifestyle change, or even just letting go of the perfectionist mentality. It forces us to let down our guard. And while it's terrifying at first, what we often find on the other side is not failure but a glimmer of freedom. The freedom to try new things, make mistakes and laugh at ourselves along the way.

When I look back at the times when I was so consumed by the fear of not being good enough, I see how much I missed out on. The constant drive to 'be the best' leaves little room for experimentation, for enjoying the process, for letting life take you by surprise. I realise now that if I had spent less time worrying about failing and more time simply embracing the unknown, I could have had so much more fun. But, as they say, it's never too late.

The beauty of confronting your fears and embracing change is that it teaches you resilience, adaptability, and perhaps most importantly, it teaches you to let go. Once you let go of the need for everything to be perfect, once you stop fearing every potential failure, you free yourself to simply live - and as it turns out, living is where the fun begins.

We often think of fun as something reserved for the carefree, for those who don't have the same worries, the same burdens. But fun isn't just for the young or the unburdened. It's for anyone willing to take risks, step outside the boundaries they've set for themselves, and embrace life's messiness. The fun doesn't come from having everything figured out, from being in control of every outcome; it comes from the moments when we allow ourselves to be surprised, to be imperfect, to be human. Like that first time, you take a leap of faith, the thrill of venturing into the unknown, the joy of realising that the world won't end just because you didn't meet some arbitrary standard. These are the moments that make life exciting. They are the moments where fear transforms into courage, where change becomes a possibility, and where you rediscover the simple pleasure of having fun just for the sake of it.

Did you face a fear today? Did you embrace a change, even if it was just trying a new recipe? Celebrate it! These small wins add up and help build your confidence for the bigger challenges. But here's the truth: most fears are just figments of your imagination. Often magnified by the pressure of societal expectations. Take a deep breath and remember that fear is a natural part of growth.

So, while fear may have its grip on us and while change can feel unsettling, it's also about having a life that isn't just filled with accomplishments and checklists but with joy, laughter, and moments that make it all worthwhile. And maybe, just maybe, it's in learning to embrace that truth that we finally learn how to have fun again.

Remember those hobbies you used to love but put aside because life got in the way? Now is the perfect time to revisit them. Whether it's painting, gardening, writing, or dancing, reconnecting with these activities can bring immense joy and satisfaction. Heading into your 40s is a chance to indulge in what makes your heart sing without worrying about whether you're perfect at it or not. The key is to find something that excites you, something that you do purely for the joy of it. Understandably so, as life gets busier and more demanding, it's easy to lose sight of what really matters. The fact is, sometimes, the most fulfilling moments are those spent in good company, where you can be yourself without any pretences. The wonderful truth is that plans don't always need to be set in stone. Allow yourself to be spontaneous, and add a refreshing sense of adventure to your life. Let go of the need for everything to be perfect and just enjoy the ride - figuratively, and heck, maybe even literally.

You may find that your social circle might start to shift. You might find yourself gravitating toward friends who share your current stage of life and who understand the challenges and triumphs you're experiencing. These friendships are invaluable. They provide support, laughter, and a sense of camaraderie that makes facing fears and embracing change a bit easier. So make time for those friends who make you laugh until you cry, who offer wise advice and a shoulder to lean on. Your tribe is your cheerleading squad, and together, you can tackle any challenge with a sense of humour and resilience. I used to believe that high school friendships were determined by the groups we fell into, the cliques, the labels, and the assumptions we made about each other based on surface-level traits. It was easy to categorise people, to think that someone wasn't "my type" of friend simply because they hung out with a different crowd, dressed differently, or shared different interests. In the bubble of adolescence, it felt like those differences defined everything. We stuck to what we knew, and our friend circles were largely shaped by perceptions of who we thought fit into our world and who didn't. Looking back now, I realise just how misguided those perceptions were, how they blinded me to potential connections that could have enriched my life much sooner.

Years later, life has a funny way of shaking those perceptions loose. As we all stepped into adulthood, faced our own challenges, and experienced the ups and downs that life inevitably brings, I found myself reconnecting with people I had once barely given a second thought to in high school. People who, at the time, seemed to be on completely different paths, with completely different values. And to my surprise, we had far more in common than I ever could have imagined. The barriers that once seemed so impenetrable, the groups we belonged to, the reputations we tried to uphold - had dissolved. What was left were the shared experiences of life that bonded us in ways that felt natural, meaningful, and genuine.

It turns out that many of those people I had written off as not "my type" back then have become some of the most integral parts of my life now. As we've grown older, we've discovered that our values, struggles, and aspirations are often more aligned than they ever appeared to be during our teenage years. We've faced similar challenges, navigating careers, relationships, families, and personal growth, and those shared experiences have brought us closer together in ways I never would have anticipated. The people who once felt like strangers now feel like lifelong friends, not because of our shared history in our high school years but because of the deep, authentic connections we've formed as adults.

It's funny how time changes everything. The very things that seemed so important back then - the cliques, the status, the desire to fit in. All seem laughably insignificant now. What truly matters is the substance of a person, not the group they were part of or the image they projected. I've come to realise that we're all just navigating the same human experience and that the people who once felt so different from me are often the ones who understand me the best.

In many ways, I regret not getting to know these people sooner. I wonder how much I missed out on by clinging to those high school perceptions, how many deep friendships I could have fostered if I had only looked beyond the surface. But at the same time, I'm grateful for the chance to reconnect now, with the wisdom and maturity to appreciate them fully. These friendships, formed later in life, are rich with understanding, support, and the kind of shared history that deepens over time. They've become some of the most important relationships in my life, and I'm constantly reminded that the people we least expect can often turn out to be the ones we need the most.

What I've learned is that we all evolve, and the people we meet along the way evolve with us. The friends I once overlooked have grown into individuals who challenge me, inspire me, and support me in ways I never anticipated. They've become part of the fabric of my life, and I can't imagine my world without them. It's a humbling reminder that first impressions are often wrong and that life has a way of bringing people back into our orbit when the time is right. When we're finally ready to see them for who they truly are, not who we assumed them to be.

We are in a time of transition, and it's okay to feel uncertain or overwhelmed. Treat yourself with the same compassion and understanding that you would offer a friend. Recognise that it's okay to have fears, to struggle with change, and to not have everything figured out. Self-compassion is a powerful tool in navigating the complexities of this stage in life.

Change is inevitable, and the sooner you embrace it, the smoother your journey will be.

As you enter this new decade, remember that fun isn't about fitting into someone else's idea of a good time. It's about finding joy in the things that make you feel alive, and that resonate with who you are now. So go ahead, embrace the changes, let go of the past, and step into your 40s with a sense of adventure and a heart open to all the fun that life still has to offer. And if that fun happens to include early bedtimes, stretchy pants, and sipping wine while rewatching old sitcoms, well, congratulations - you've officially made it.

Chapter 14

Getting Schooled

Lesson Plans: How to Lose Arguments to a 6-Year-Old

Let's start with the fact that I still consider myself young-ish – you know, the young where you can still hang out with the cool kids but also complain about back pain when you stand up too fast. It's an odd middle ground where you're balancing nostalgia for your carefree days with the harsh realities of adulthood. And with that sense of "youth" you're still clinging onto comes the ridiculous habit of treating everyone older than yourself like some kind of wise oracle. It's like I've been conditioned to think that anyone with a few more years under their belt is a walking fortune cookie of life advice. But guess what? They're not. Most of the time, they're just winging it too. And here's the kicker – I need to remind myself that I am actually no longer a kid. I'm a grown-ass adult, and it's high time I stepped out of this weird hierarchy where I assume everyone knows better than me. Cause they probably don't.

Maybe this lack of confidence comes from being the eldest child, the one who had to "pave the way" and go through all the terrifying firsts – first in line for school, first to mess up, first to disappoint. Or maybe it's because I was the "new kid" one too many times, moving around so much that by the time I finally made a friend, I'd already packed up ready to leave again. Who knows? All I know is that those early experiences shape the way we see ourselves in relation to others, often in ways we don't fully recognise until much later. It could also be that classic generational trait we all inherited – the fine art of self-doubt, handed down like an old family recipe no one wanted.

Then I look at the kids these days, these pint-sized humans who seem to have been born with Wi-Fi and a fully functioning sense of confidence built in. Where did they get that? Was it in the water? Why didn't they have to fight tooth and nail for it the way my contemporaries and I had to? Because I swear, these kids are not here to play nice and follow the rules. They're here to challenge everything, question everyone, and tell you exactly what they think without a second thought. They don't care if you're their elder or if you've got a decade of experience with them. They will tell you you're wrong and probably tweet about it.

But that's the thing: they're not weighed down by the same deference that kept me and you shackled for so long. They don't care if you've got more candles on your birthday cake; they care about whether you've got something worth listening to. And sometimes, I envy their audacity, their ability to live in a world where "because I said so" just doesn't cut it anymore. There's a sort of freedom in that mindset, a willingness to call things as they see them and not be afraid of the repercussions. It's both terrifying and inspiring, really.

Preteens have traditionally been all about distancing themselves from anything that feels "too kiddish" – think Disney shows, toys, and the like. But Gen Alpha is rewriting that narrative in surprising ways. I'm learning that this latest generation is an entirely different breed. They are less prone to peer pressure and more supportive of individuality. They don't care if they come across as too kiddish because, to them, being kiddish isn't a bad thing. It's freeing!

Take something like Friday the 13th. For us, it was the ultimate omen of bad luck, a day synonymous with superstitions and horror. I wouldn't have dared to even breathe too hard on a Friday the 13th back in the day. My friends and I would practically tiptoe through the day, avoiding black cats and ladders like our lives depended on it. But for Gen Alpha? It's just another countdown to Taylor Swift's birthday. This generation doesn't get caught up in old-school fears or outdated superstitions. Instead, they find joy in celebrating what matters to them, unbothered by the traditional hang-ups we used to carry. It's truly admirable. Their priorities are different, and that's refreshing. It makes me wonder what other traditions and norms they'll throw out the window as they grow older.

A few nights ago, Abby and I were having one of our famous bedtime chats. You know, the ones where the school gossip flows freely, and you find out more about playground politics than you'd ever care to know. I've always prided myself on being a "cool mom," the kind who listens, nods, and occasionally throws in a nugget of motherly wisdom. But that night, the conversation took a turn. Abby, my sweet little angel, casually dropped the bomb that she might not make the tennis team because someone else (who didn't even try out) had. Naturally, my inner mama bear started stretching, ready to get frisky.

I jumped into action mode, fully prepared to send a strongly worded email to whoever would listen to my rant about fairness. But before I could even hit 'send,' Abby, with all the calm of a Zen master, looked at me and said, "Mom, maybe we should think about this before doing anything." I blinked, stunned. Was this the same child who used to throw a fit when she couldn't find her favourite stuffed animal?

There I was, about to go all-out Mama Bear mode, and my nine-year-old was schooling me on emotional restraint. It was like I'd been transported into a parenting alternate universe where my kid is the one with the cool head, and I'm the one acting like I've lost my juice box. It was like the student had truly become the teacher, and I, the teacher, was being sent to the corner to reflect on my behaviour. I suddenly had the urge to go sit in time-out. It hit me then – how often do we, as parents, assume we know best simply because we're the adults? Sometimes, the wisdom we think we possess pales in comparison to the calm insight our kids can offer in an unexpected moment.

I had to laugh because what else could I do? Here was my child, handling disappointment like a seasoned diplomat, while I was one minor inconvenience away from starting a Change.org petition. Instead of raging at the world, she was calm, rational, and completely unbothered by the trivial dramas that once consumed my life at her age. And at that moment, I realised that Abby had become my greatest teacher.

All those years of parenting, trying to impart wisdom, teach her to be brave, to speak up, to know her worth, had somehow come full circle. Now, it was Abby who was reminding me of those lessons and making me see that perhaps I had some growing up to do myself.

I mean, isn't that what parenting is all about? We start out thinking we're shaping these little beings into better versions of themselves, only to find out that they've been stealthily reverse-mentoring us the whole time showing us how to live better, think smarter, and occasionally tell our inner psycho mom to take a chill pill. It's a humbling realisation but one that makes the journey that much richer.

And so, as I sat there on the edge of her bed, marvelling at how far we've both come, I had to admit that while I'm supposed to be the adult, it's okay to learn from my kid. It's okay to let her lead the way sometimes, to show me that not every battle needs to be fought, and not every injustice needs a full-on letter-writing campaign. Sometimes, the letter can wait while you eat a cookie and work on your 'emotional regulation'.

In the end, life isn't about who's older or wiser, it's about who's willing to learn, evolve, and let go of the old playbook. In fact, I think it's time we stopped handing down that old playbook at all; nobody really wants or needs it! And sometimes, just sometimes, the best teacher you'll ever have is sitting right across from you, wearing a unicorn onesie, and reminding you to calm the heck down.

Chapter 15

Unsubscribing from Stress

The Power of No and Letting Go

I'm a woman who could best be described as "chronically agreeable." If there was an award for saying "yes" to absolutely everything, I would have a trophy case full of them. Need someone to take you to the salon because your car was taken in for a service? Don't bother to call Uber, call Ally. Want someone to bake 100 cupcakes for the school fundraiser she's not even a part of? Ally's your girl. Oh, and don't forget the time I agreed to join a boxing class at 6 a.m., even though I had absolutely no intention of ever showing up. But, in true Ally fashion, I would always say "yes" with a smile.

Saying "no" wasn't in my vocabulary - until one day, the universe decided to give me a not-so-subtle nudge. And by nudge, I mean a full-blown shove.

It all started when I foolishly agreed to plan a friend's baby shower, organise my office's year-end party, volunteer at my kid's school family day, and also help my mother-in-law redecorate her living room - all in the same week. Honestly, what was I thinking? By Thursday, I was running on nothing but caffeine, sheer panic, and the kind of adrenaline rush you get when you're being chased by a monkey. I caught a glimpse of myself in the bathroom mirror and, for a brief, horrifying moment, thought, 'holy hell, I look like a sleep-deprived extra from a zombie apocalypse movie'. I could practically hear a voiceover saying, "And this is what happens when you say yes to everything."

The insanity behind my haggard appearance wasn't just the to-do list from hell - it was the fact that I felt obligated to keep saying "YES" to absolutely everything. I was a professional yes-woman, a human Swiss Army knife if you may, ready to bend and fold myself into any shape just to keep everyone happy.

Until one fateful morning when I found myself standing in the kitchen, sobbing over a burnt batch of eggless cupcakes (because my life wasn't chaotic enough without dietary restrictions); these cupcakes were, of course, for a friend. The smoke alarm was blaring like a banshee; my phone was buzzing with a school pickup reminder that was just 15 minutes away, and suddenly - like a brick to the face -it hit me: I had officially lost control of my life.

In that exact moment, in the midst of burnt-cupcake despair, something inside me snapped - or maybe it was more like a click, like that old-school light bulb finally flickering on. I tossed the spatula onto the counter (with more drama than was probably necessary), silenced the alarm, and with a voice that was a mix of exhaustion, rage, and newfound clarity, I muttered, "I'm done. I'm saying NO."

Cue the clouds parting, a beam of light shining down, and angels singing, "Hallelujah!" I was reborn.

Fuelled by a potent mix of frustration and flour-covered rebellion, I whipped out my phone and began texting with the ferocity of a woman who had finally lost it. "Sorry, I can't make it to family day." "I'll have to tap out on the redecorating for now." "Baby shower? I'll help, but I'm not doing it all!" I was texting "no" with such vengeance that I thought my thumbs might fall off. But with every message, I felt lighter and freer. For the first time in my life, I was actively saying no - and guess what? The world didn't explode. People didn't hate me. No one organised a pitchfork-wielding mob to come after me. In fact, shockingly, people respected me for it.

Who knew "no" could be so empowering?

But the real turning point came later that week when my client (who had a knack for dumping last-minute projects on my desk like I was her personal workhorse) waltzed in with another "urgent" task. Normally, I would've smiled through the internal panic, said yes, and mentally prepared for another all-nighter fuelled by coffee and regret. But this time? This time, I took a deep breath, squared my shoulders, and calmly said, "No, unfortunately, I won't be able to get that done today."

Her reaction? Absolute shock. However, instead of pushing back or having an attitude, she simply blinked, nodded, and said, "Okay, no problem. I'll find someone else."

And that was it. No drama, no bitchiness, no guilt, no catastrophic consequences. My "no" was received as a casual weather update. Initial surprise, but - Life. Went. On.

As I left the office that day, something remarkable happened: I realised I didn't just have the power to say no - I had the power to let go. Let go of the need to be everything to everyone. Let go of the irrational fear that the world would fall apart if I didn't step in. Let go of the guilt I'd been carrying around for years, thinking that prioritising myself made me selfish. And in letting go, I found something I hadn't experienced in ages: peace. Sweet, blissful, unburdened peace.

That weekend, I lay out on my couch with a glass of wine in one hand (a drink I didn't have to share) and my phone blissfully silent. No reminders, no tasks, no obligations. Just me, the couch, and my new friend - Mrs Icansayno.
Sure, I could've filled my schedule with a dozen more things, but this moment? This moment of freedom and complete, glorious laziness? This was exactly what I'd been missing all along.

The power of "no" wasn't just about setting boundaries with other people - it was about setting boundaries with myself. It was learning that I didn't have to prove my worth through endless commitments and ridiculous expectations. And that letting go didn't make me weak - it made me wise.

And, dare I say it, it made life a whole lot better.

So, my days of being the human 'yes' button are officially behind me. I've discovered the magic of "no," and trust me, there's no going back. Well... unless brunch is involved. Let's not get crazy - no one says no to brunch.

• • •

The art of letting go. It sounds so serene and zen, doesn't it? But in reality, it often feels like trying to untangle a massive knot in a string of holiday lights - frustrating, messy, and filled with the occasional burst of exasperation. But let's face it: holding on to old grudges, outdated expectations, and things that no longer serve us is like carrying around a backpack filled with rocks. And who needs that kind of weight when you're headed towards your fabulous 40s?

Let's start with holding onto the past. Where all our best and worst memories live, usually with a sprinkling of regret and nostalgia. Sure, it's tempting to replay those moments where you wished you'd said something snappier at the rude woman with a sharp tongue or where you didn't quite hit the high note at karaoke. But here's a little secret: the past is a fantastic place to visit but a terrible place to live.

The truth is that the grudges you hold might have meant something once, but they're not worth clinging to. Another case of 'easier said than done', right? Trust me, I know this all too well. I've been through hell with someone who is close to me. Often, I wonder why this person is still in my life after treating me the way they did. When I occasionally get reminded of the situation I was put through, I'm lucky enough to have Roux, who reminds me to ask myself if it's benefitting me in any way to hold on to this grudge. Is it hurting me or that other person? The fact is, it's always hurting me more. Purely because the other person was pretty oblivious and probably wasn't as affected as I was during that time in my life. So yes, whilst theoretically, I know I need to let go, I endeavour to do so every time I get reminded. Not because I want to appear unaffected. But because my mental health is more important than that person, I refuse to give them the power to make me feel bad about myself. If anything, that's a good enough reason right there. No one is worth your emotional well-being - not even someone who once seemed like an immovable force in your life. So, why do we hold on to these grudges like they're family heirlooms? We need to stop clinging to a sweater that's three sizes too small. Just face it, it used to fit, maybe even look great, but now it's just suffocating you. And yet, we keep it in the back of the closet 'just in case' - as if we're ever going to wear it again. Fun Fact: we never will.

The thing is, grudges don't just keep you stuck in the past, they actively block your future. They take up valuable real estate in your mind, rent-free, while you're paying the emotional price. And the person you're stewing over? They're likely off somewhere blissfully unaware, living their life, unbothered by the mental space they're occupying in your head.

That's when it hits you: letting go isn't about forgiving them for what they did - it's about freeing yourself from the weight of carrying it. It's about reclaiming your peace, your energy, and your sanity. The way I see it is that we have to rely on one another to continue to remind each other to LET GO. Because life is too short to let anyone, especially someone who isn't even thinking about you, steal your joy. So, the next time someone tries to rain on your parade, just grab an umbrella, do a little dance, and remind them that their negativity can't spoil your sunny disposition!

Chapter 16

Green Smoothies & Om-lettes

Namaste, But Make It Quick

As I inch closer to 40, a strange phenomenon has started happening: everyone keeps telling me that I need to focus on my "health and spirituality." It's like there's some cosmic memo that gets circulated once you hit 39. Suddenly, I'm bombarded with unsolicited advice from people who have apparently all become enlightened overnight or, at the very least, have bought a yoga mat and some sage.

"Oh, you're almost 40?" they say with wide-eyed concern. "You should really think about cutting down on caffeine and sugar." Cut down?? I can barely keep up with the demands of my life, with those two substances fuelling me. And don't even get me started on how they casually drop the idea of meditating as I can just sit still for 20 minutes and "clear my mind." My mind is a circus on the best of days. Twenty minutes of silence is basically an invitation for my brain to replay every awkward moment from the past 25 years, complete with a detailed analysis of why I ever did what I did.

And yet, here I am, trying to be the best version of myself as I stare 40 in the face, squinting (thanks to my diminishing eyesight) to see if it really is all downhill from here or if there's some wisdom in all this health and spirituality talk. The truth is, I have dabbled. I went to a hot yoga class once, which, for those unfamiliar, is essentially like trying to do stretches inside a human-sized oven. I was dripping with sweat while everyone else in the room appeared to be glistening like serene, bendy goddesses. As I flailed around trying to get into something called "downward dog," I couldn't help but wonder if the yoga instructor was secretly punishing us for past sins.

As for spirituality, I've tried meditating. Sort of. Okay, fine, I downloaded a meditation app. I opened it once, and then I got distracted by Instagram. But hey, it's the thought that counts, right? I mean, I'm really trying to be more mindful, but every time I sit down to meditate, my brain is like, "Hey, remember that embarrassing thing you did in high school? Let's think about that for the next 10 minutes." And before I know it, I'm spiralling into a black hole of cringe-worthy memories while pretending to be zen.

I think the problem is that no one tells you that trying to be healthy and spiritual is a process. Like, it doesn't just happen because you turned 40 and suddenly got hit with a wave of motivation. It's more like a series of tiny, often ridiculous steps that sometimes make you question whether you're improving yourself or just becoming a parody of a wellness influencer.

Case in point: I decided to cleanse my aura. Apparently, it was "clogged" and needed some TLC. So, I bought some sage because, I've been told, that's what you do. I lit it, waved it around the house, and accidentally set off the smoke alarm. My husband thought I was trying to burn down the kitchen, again, and my daughter asked if we were having a barbecue. I wasn't sure if my aura got cleansed, but my living room smelled like a forest fire for a solid week. So, there's that.

And let's not forget the juicing phase. Oh yes, because apparently, turning 40 also means you must now consume kale in liquid form. I bought a fancy juicer, spent a fortune on organic vegetables, and tried to convince myself that I actually liked the taste of celery. I, in fact, did not like the taste of celery. After a week of pretending that I was "totally into juicing," I gave up and went back to my beloved coffee because I stand firm on this: life is too short to drink liquefied grass.

The truth is, once you start to see that your Instagram feed is shifting from serving you content about loungewear to manifestation and once it starts preaching about how the universe has your back. You then somehow find yourself contemplating a lot more on which anti-wrinkle cream to invest in or how to keep your energy levels up with a chaotic schedule. What has struck me most is the intertwining of health and spirituality, two areas of life I hadn't previously considered together. But now, as I navigate this new chapter, I see them as inseparable - two sides of the same coin that are critical to not just surviving my 40s but thriving in them.

Let's start with health, the more tangible of the two. For much of my 20s and 30s, I lived under the comforting delusion that my body was invincible.

There were years of late-night takeouts, the ingrained perception that workouts were not for me, and too many weekends indulging in alcoholic beverages and various series of marathons. And sure, I had some vague notion that one day I'd need to "get serious" about my health, but I always thought that day was years away. After all, I still fit into my jeans and managed to function well enough on five hours of sleep, so as far as I knew, I was totally fine.

As I inch forward in life, my body has made it abundantly clear that it's time for me to shape up, literally and figuratively. My metabolism has slowed, I need more sleep than ever before, and let's just say my body has started to respond a lot less kindly to poor food choices. The old aches and pains I'd previously ignored are now daily reminders that my body is asking for more attention and care.

But here's the thing. It's not just about physical fitness or losing the "extra padding" that's crept up over the years. It's about a more profound understanding of my health as something deeply holistic. This isn't just about maintaining a certain weight or adhering to strict diets; it's about nurturing every part of me: mind, body, and soul. I started to notice something else, too. Stress - whether from work, relationships, or life's many curveballs - was having a tangible effect on my body. My immune system wasn't as strong, I'd get frequent headaches, and my digestion seemed to rebel every time I let stress take the driver's seat. These signs pointed to something I had neglected for far too long. Dear readers, that is a fascinating connection between the mind and body.

I realised I couldn't just "eat healthily" or "work out more" and call it a day. True health, I found, isn't just about what you're doing - it's about how you're living. This leads me to the second part of this journey: spirituality.

For many years, spirituality wasn't really on my radar. Sure, I tried out a couple of yoga classes, downloaded the occasional mindfulness app, and had fleeting moments of reflection. But it was always something that felt...optional. Like, "I'll get to that when I have time." Truth be told, I never really had time.

But recently, something shifted. The noise of everyday life, career demands, family obligations, and societal expectations all began to feel overwhelming. I understood that I needed something deeper, something grounding, to navigate it all. Cue the discovery of spirituality, not in a religious sense, but in the form of a personal journey of inner peace.

What surprised me most is that spirituality doesn't require a pilgrimage to a mountaintop or hours spent meditating in silence (though those sound nice too!). It can be as simple as taking a few minutes each day to breathe deeply and acknowledge where I am, mentally and emotionally. It's about reconnecting with my inner self and recognising that my health is not just about how my body feels but how my spirit feels.

And what I've found is that this spiritual grounding has had an incredible effect on my overall well-being. As I've become more mindful and present in my daily life, I've noticed that my body responds in kind. Stress doesn't hit me as hard, I sleep better, and I have more energy - not just the physical kind, but the emotional and spiritual kind, too.

The connection between health and spirituality became crystal clear the day I found myself sitting in the doctor's office, hearing that very common-in-a-woman-world phrase: "You need to reduce your stress levels." Sure, who doesn't? This wasn't news to me, but hearing it from a medical professional felt like perhaps I should take it seriously and consider it a bit of a wake-up call. I'd always known, on some level, that my stress was taking a toll on my health, but I had compartmentalised it, believing I could handle it all.

Turns out I couldn't.

I've since learned that true health cannot exist without spirituality, and vice versa. I needed to heal not just my body but my mind and spirit as well. This realisation has transformed how I consider and think about everything, from the food I eat to the workouts I do to the way I handle difficult situations in life. I now understand that I can't just run on autopilot, checking off tasks and meeting everyone's needs but my own.

I must note that it's by no means an easy fix. It requires work. Mostly mental work. It's about getting your mind to agree to this shift and, more importantly, commit to this shift. Sure, there will be days and times when you feel overwhelmed, and you want to indulge in a bit of nonmental, nonspiritual antics - and that's ok, too. So long as you come back to the shift and continue practicing both body and mind health.

I try to play Padel and consider it not just a form of exercise but a way to centre myself. I try to meditate, not because I want to achieve some lofty state of zen, but because it sometimes helps me quiet the constant chatter in my mind and listen to what my body tells me. I've even started writing more, something I once considered a waste of time but now see as a vital tool for processing emotions and staying in tune with myself. I started, and I occasionally stopped practicing regular gratitude and setting intentions. Life is hard; it is not easy to always be vibrating at high frequencies. However, in my opinion, that's ok. So long as you have something you can turn to that will help ground you again, and that is when you will be able to find your peace. I personally used to think gratitude was just something people wrote about in self-help books, but let me tell you, it's a game-changer.

I read this book by Gabby Bernstein called Super Attractor. If you have not read it, I suggest you do. In it, she teaches that you have the power to manifest a life filled with purpose and joy. By aligning with the universe, trusting your intuition, and releasing control, you can attract the happiness, love, and abundance you desire. It's about embracing a mindset of positivity and allowing yourself to find peace and security in that space. It's a space you can turn to when you need to feel grounded.

Every morning, before I dive into the chaos of my day, I take a moment to reflect on what I'm grateful for. It doesn't have to be anything grand; sometimes, it's as simple as appreciating a quiet moment with my morning coffee, feeling the sun on my face, or admiring my beautiful white and cream bougainvilleas. But even with these small acts of gratitude, I find it has the power to shift my entire mindset. Instead of focusing on what's going wrong or what I have on my to-do list, I find myself starting the day on a positive, centred note regardless if it all goes to shit come to the peak of school-run morning mayhem.

And then there's intention. I mostly live by the clock, racing from one task to the next, but now I've made a conscious effort to live with intention. That means slowing down, paying attention, and asking myself 'why'. Why am I pushing myself so hard at work? Why am I saying yes to that social event when I'd rather have a quiet night? By questioning my actions and intentions, I've started making decisions that align with my health, both physically and spiritually.

Approaching 40 has forced me to pay attention not just to my body but to my mind, my soul, and what I actually need. Sure, I joke about yoga and sage and kale, but deep down, I know that this whole "turning 40" business is about more than just trying to squeeze into skinny jeans or mastering downward dog. It's about finding balance. The balance between laughing at myself and taking care of myself. So here I am, embracing this holistic approach to health and spirituality; I've found a new sense of freedom. I don't have to choose between being fit and being centred, between caring for my body and nurturing my spirit. I can and should do both. As I step into this next chapter of my life, I begin to understand that my 40s aren't about slowing down or giving in to the pressures of aging; they're about stepping into my power, my health, and my spirituality.

I may not be a meditation master, but I've learned how to take a deep breath when life feels overwhelming. I may never love kale, but I've found a version of healthy eating that doesn't make me miserable. And while I might not be waving crystals around with any regularity, I'm learning to let go of the things that don't serve me - and that, dear reader, is its own kind of spirituality.

So, as I approach this next chapter of life, I'm embracing my health and spirituality journey - flawed, funny, and far from perfect. Because, at the end of the day, isn't that what life is all about? Finding the humour in the chaos, the peace in the imperfection, and maybe, just maybe, a little bit of wisdom along the way.

Namaste.

Chapter 17

Redefining Success

Because Apparently, Glitter Doesn't Grow on Trees

There's an expectation that as you grow older, your definition of success should naturally evolve. It's almost like there's an invisible checklist for adulthood: by 40, you should have this, this, and this. But life isn't that neat and tidy, is it? Success at this stage is as much about managing expectations as it is about achieving goals. Maybe you didn't hit all the markers you set for yourself at 25, and that's okay. Perhaps the dream job turned out to be less dreamy, or the 'perfect' relationship wasn't so perfect after all. But here's the thing: success is also about resilience - about how you pick yourself up, dust yourself off, and keep going, even when the plan changes.

And let's be real – the plan always changes, doesn't it? There's that inevitable moment when life throws you a curveball, and you're left standing there, hands up in the air, thinking, "Well, that wasn't in the brochure." But maybe that's where the real magic happens – in the unplanned, the unexpected. Because as much as you might prefer it, you can't just stick to the script. Success is about improvising, ad-libbing, and sometimes even writing a brand-new script altogether. Heck, just burn the script while you're at it because you might not even end up using it!

In your 20s, success might have been defined by the size of your paycheck, the prestige of your job title, or the speed at which you could climb the corporate ladder in your very expensive but much-needed heels. But as you navigate through your late 30s, you begin to see that the goalposts have moved, and suddenly, success looks a lot different than it did a decade ago.

There's an unspoken expectation that as you mature, your definition of success should evolve too. It's almost as if society gives you a gentle (or sometimes not-so-gentle) nudge to start reevaluating what truly matters. The question is, are you ready for that shift?

It definitely took me time to accept this mental shift. But when it hit in, it hit hard. Reality set, and you realise the plain and simple truth - that life is too short.

Here's a slight deviation but one that I believe has a silver lining on this topic: My Dad died suddenly when he was 55 years old. At the time of utter devastation, the idea of 'life being too short' had a generic sort of meaning. The fact is that when someone's life comes to an end so suddenly, you cannot help but re-evaluate your time. How much of if you have left? What have you done with your time thus far? And my most favourite ponder: how will you spend your time going forward, unknowing when times-up?

Heading into the next decade and considering the number 55 – it's a scary thought because it's a lot closer to the number 40 than I can believe.

This is a rather sobering thought and one I would not like to spend too much time on. The outcome has me reflecting a little longer in front of the mirror every morning, wondering and questioning if I'm truly living the life I want to live or not. But here's the kicker - instead of living in fear of time, I've decided to treat it as a daily challenge and wake-up call to live life deliberately. And this acceptance is a redefinition of success in my eyes.

So, when pulling together this chapter, I found some themes that I think are really important to highlight when it comes to redefining success. And here they are:

1. Success is No Longer Just About the Hustle

Remember those days when success was all about the hustle? You wore your busyness like a badge of honour, filling every waking hour with meetings, deadlines, and to-do lists. Any moment of rest was a moment wasted, and you couldn't waste a moment if you were chasing success single-mindedly. But as you get older, you start to comprehend that constantly being 'on' isn't sustainable - or even desirable. Success begins to take on a new meaning, one that involves balance, well-being, and, dare I say it, enjoying life. It's about finding that sweet spot where your career, relationships, and personal growth all coexist in harmony. Success is no longer just about how much you can achieve but how well you can live.

2. Redefine Success by Your Own Standards

In your 20s and early 30s, success often feels like a race - one where you're constantly comparing yourself to others. Who's got the better job? Who's buying a house? Who's getting married, having kids, or achieving that picture-perfect life we all think we should want? But as you inch closer to 40, you start to grasp that success isn't a one-size-fits-all concept. It's not about keeping up with the Joneses (whoever they are) but about defining what success means to you. Maybe it's about finally pursuing that passion project, or perhaps it's about taking a step back to focus on your mental health and happiness. Whatever it is, it's yours, and that's what makes it successful.

This redefinition is personal, intimate even. It can be uncomfortable at first – to no longer use others as benchmarks for your own progress. There's a certain freedom in it, though. When you finally realise that success looks different for everyone, you give yourself the space to succeed on your own terms. And maybe that's what growing older is all about – not chasing someone else's idea of achievement but building your own. You might even realise that you're not running the same race anymore. You're at an altogether different event.

3. Success is not a destination - It's a Journey

One of the biggest shifts that happens as you near 40 is the understanding that success isn't a final destination. There's no point where you suddenly 'arrive' and everything is perfect. Instead, success is a journey, a series of milestones that you reach at your own pace. It's about growth, learning, and adapting to the changes life throws your way. And sometimes, the most successful moments are the ones that come from unexpected detours when you understand that the path you're on is exactly where you need to be.

As you get closer to 40, you may find that success isn't just about what you gain but also about what you let go of. It's about releasing the pressure to have it all figured out, the need to meet everyone's expectations, and the fear of not being 'enough.' Sometimes, the most successful thing you can do is to give yourself permission to change your mind, to pursue a different path, or to simply say, "I don't need this anymore." It's liberating, and it's a sign of true growth.

And that liberation? It's powerful. It's the moment you stop running towards something that doesn't serve you anymore and start walking at your own pace in a direction that feels right for you. That's a different kind of success – one that doesn't come with applause or trophies but brings a quiet, unshakeable peace to your mind and soul.

You start to appreciate the small victories just as much as the big ones. Sometimes, success is the quiet moments - the decision to take care of yourself, the time spent with loved ones, or the courage to make a change - that define your success. Celebrate those moments. They're just as important as the big milestones, if not more so.

Success isn't measured by the accolades you collect but by the joy, growth, and fulfilment you experience along the way.

As you redefine what success means in your life, remember that it's a deeply personal journey. It's not about meeting anyone else's expectations but about finding what truly makes you feel accomplished, content, and fulfilled. Whether that means chasing new dreams or savouring the life you've built, success is what you decide it to be. So go ahead, redefine it - on your terms.

Storytime: A friend of mine, Vicky, is the kind of mom who manages to juggle work calls, homework help, and dinner prep, all while looking like she just stepped out of a magazine...well, most days, anyway. But even the finest jugglers drop the ball sometimes. One fateful Monday morning, in her whirlwind of multi-tasking brilliance, she confidently strode into the school drop-off looking like a million bucks. Except for one minor detail: her boots. She had somehow managed to slip on one sleek black ankle boot and one chunky brown boot, turning her morning school run into a fashion faux pas worthy of its own reality show. As the other parents did double-takes, Vicky just laughed it off, declaring, "Today, I'm redefining success! Who needs matching boots when I've managed to get my kids to school on time?" We laughed, not because we thought she was a nutcase, but because we totally 'got it'. Her crazy was every bit my crazy, too. And dare I will be so bold as to say; it was damn well every other mom's crazy as well. Because, let's be honest, in the grand scheme of things, nailing the perfect pair of boots pales in comparison to the epic balancing act of being a working mom and wife. If success means wearing two different boots, then I love Vicky even more for proudly walking her own runway, one mismatched step at a time!

In today's world, where every Instagram highlight reel often makes us feel various levels of inadequacy, Vicky was a refreshing reminder that sometimes, it's the little blunders that truly unite us. After all, if she could waltz through life with one boot in style and another in complete chaos, then maybe the real measure of success isn't in matching footwear but in finding joy in the delightful messiness of motherhood, adulthood, and womanhood. Another good friend of ours, Nicole, dropped some wisdom the other day that stuck with me like a stubborn piece of confetti on a party hat. She said, "My friend, there's nothing better than being a Fruit Loop in a world full of Cheerios." And honestly, I can't think of a better way to wrap up this chapter than with her colourful reminder to embrace our unique perspectives on success.

Drop Mic BOOM*

Chapter 18

The Bucketlist Bonanza

And it's Silver Lining

It all starts innocently enough. You're sitting at your favourite coffee shop, feeling inspired after reading an article about self-fulfilment and the importance of a bucket list. "I need to live life to the fullest!" you declare, probably to a bemused barista. You jot down grand plans, like learning to Salsa in Buenos Aires, hiking the Inca Trail, or writing a novel that'll rival J.K. Rowling. It's the stuff of dreams. Your list is a sparkling testament to all the amazing things you're going to achieve, and it's going to make your life an epic saga of awesomeness.

Fast forward to a few months later, and suddenly, your bucket list is a hilarious testament to the gap between ambition and reality. Take, for example, the time you decided to follow through and learn to salsa. You envisioned a glamorous dance floor, your feet gigging to the beat of the floor.

In reality, you spent most of the lesson tripping over your partner's feet and awkwardly apologising to the instructor, who seemed to be silently questioning your commitment to the art of dance. The salsa lessons are still on the list, now marked with a few doodles and the note: "Maybe next year?!?"

Or perhaps your grand idea was to master the art of gourmet cooking. You imagined yourself whipping up five-star meals with the ease of a Michelin-starred chef. What actually happened was an unexpected fire alarm, a very confused dog, and a kitchen that looked like it had been hit by a tornado. The kitchen disaster has since become a family legend, and the only thing you've mastered is ordering takeout with a flair.

But here's the thing: even as your bucket list items morph into humorous footnotes, there's a certain charm to the process. There's joy in the attempts, the missteps, and the eventual acceptance that maybe you're not destined to become a Step-Up dancer or a world-class chef. The beauty lies in the journey, not in the perfection of the list.

• • •

As I attempted to check in for our flight to Turkey, my cousin was on the phone, multitasking like a pro and checking in for himself and his wife while guiding me through my own check-in. It seemed foolproof, like a well-oiled machine of efficiency. After all, what could go wrong with a little synchronised clicking? But hindsight, as they say, is 20/20, and what seemed like a brilliant plan quickly revealed itself to be anything but. I had naively relied on his voice, believing that his verbal assurances could somehow magically align with my screen's demands. Now, looking back, it seems almost comically absurd, like trusting a blindfolded guide through a minefield.

Yet, life has a funny way of turning these seemingly dire moments into unexpected blessings - perhaps an unexpected outcome wrapped in a lesson. It reminds me of Alanis Morissette's tale of Mr. Play-It-Safe: the man who spent his life avoiding risks, only to finally board a plane and meet his ironic end. Just like that, my little misstep became a lesson in the absurdity of life's ironies and the hidden opportunities within them. In the end, what feels like a crash landing might just be the cosmic wink we didn't know we needed.

The utterly amateur error I made meant us departing an entire day before we had booked and planned to, due to some free-change option I had unknowingly clicked on. I probably subconsciously clicked on it when I saw the word "Free".
So there we were, after making many calls all around the world in the hope that someone from Turkish Airlines would allow me the simple task of reverting my error back to the original plan. We had no such luck.
Roux and I were now on the next flight to Istanbul and, subsequently, Cappadocia, Turkey. From the airport lounge, we were still booking accommodation for the unplanned night, booking transfers and adjusting my visa date, etc. It was what South Africans like to call real "gemors"! (Google it)

Originally, the plan included spending a magical night in Cappadocia, setting the alarm for the ungodly hour of 3 a.m. to embark on a hot air balloon adventure, a quintessential experience that graces many a bucket list. However, fate dealt us an unexpected boon: Roux and I found ourselves with an extra day sans the usual entourage. So, with an additional morning at our disposal, we chose to rise with the dawn anyway, just to witness the mesmerising ascent of the balloons from the ground. And my word, they were nothing short of breathtaking.

As the first rays of sunlight began to paint the sky in hues of pink and gold, we stood in awe, watching as dozens of vibrant balloons slowly filled with air, their massive forms rising gracefully above the fairy chimneys that dotted the otherworldly landscape. The entire scene felt like something out of a dream, with the ancient rock formations casting long shadows in the early morning light while the balloons, each one more colourful than the last, floated silently above, their reflections shimmering on the dew-kissed valleys below.

There was something profoundly beautiful and humbling about watching these gentle giants drift through the sky, almost as if they were part of some grand, choreographed ballet performed just for us. The way they moved so effortlessly and serenely against the backdrop of Cappadocia's surreal terrain, was a sight to behold, one that words can hardly do justice. It was as though time stood still, and for a few precious moments, we were completely encapsulated in the sheer magic of it all. It was an experience that fed the soul, a reminder of the simple yet profound wonders that exist in this world, waiting to be discovered by those who rise early enough to witness them. I'm forever grateful for having that precious experience with Roux.

What was even more exciting to look forward to was the following morning, when we were all set to embark on our own adventure, floating amongst these magical balloons. After witnessing the spectacle from below, our imaginations ran wild with the thought of experiencing this mystery from above - what I could imagine being like seeing the world unfold beneath us like a patchwork quilt, with the fairy chimneys and valleys stretching out as far as the eye could see.

So, here we were, the next morning, 3 a.m. - bleary-eyed but buzzing with anticipation. We got all dolled up (Instagram-worthy, of course), popped some anti-nausea meds just to be safe, downed a couple of espressos to kickstart our spirits, and made our fancy way to the fancy reception, ready to tick this experience off our bucket lists. The excitement was palpable. We could almost feel the thrill of the ascent, the rush of what that cool morning air would be like as we rose higher and higher above the ethereal landscape.

But then, as we arrived at the reception, the mood shifted. The staff, with sympathetic smiles, delivered the news that no one ever wants to hear: the hot air balloon flights had been canceled due to poor weather conditions. A sudden drop of disappointment hit like a stone in the pit of our stomachs. All that buildup, all the excitement, and just like that, the dream of soaring above Cappadocia was grounded. It felt like a cruel twist of fate - so close, yet so far from experiencing the magic we had been so eagerly anticipating.

However, in the midst of our disappointment, we couldn't help but reflect on how incredibly fortunate Roux and I had been the day before. While we may have missed the chance to glide above the fairy chimneys, we had already witnessed something truly special. Seeing those balloons rise from the ground, floating gracefully into the dawn sky, was an experience in itself

- a moment of pure, unfiltered wonder that few get to see from that perspective. Though we didn't get to be part of the spectacle from the skies, we had still been touched by its magic from below, and in that, we found a silver lining. Sometimes, the universe has a way of reminding us that the beauty of life isn't just in the grand moments we plan but in the unexpected ones we stumble upon along the way.

• • •

As you continue through your late 30s, you might find your bucket list expanding in unexpected ways. What started as a list of high-flying ambitions has now taken on a life of its own. There are new entries like "a Girl's Trip to New York" and "Master the art of making the perfect cup of coffee." These additions might not have been on your original list, but they bring a different kind of satisfaction.

In the end, your bucket list will likely evolve into a colourful painting of experiences - both grand and hilariously mundane. It's a reflection of your journey, a reminder that life isn't always about ticking off items but about enjoying the ride. Whether you're conquering mountaintops or mastering the art of making the perfect avocado on toast, the list becomes a cherished record of your adventures and misadventures.

So, embrace the quirks, the unexpected turns, and the delightful absurdities of your bucket list. It's a testament to your enthusiasm, creativity, and perhaps the ability to laugh at yourself. After all, isn't that what makes the journey truly unforgettable?

Closing thought: a bucket list is like a GPS for your dreams - sometimes it takes you on the scenic route, and sometimes it's just trying to get you to the nearest coffee shop. Whatever it is, the end result is a delightful concoction of memories that's uniquely yours!

Chapter 19

Tick Tock

Counting Blessings, Not Just Minutes

I have been truly blessed in my life. I have an amazing family, albeit we have our own dramas, as does everyone. I have had the blessing of being able to travel and live abroad. I have a beautiful home and a loving heart. What more could I ask for? As a generation, we have evolved from wanting to appreciating. From comparing to supporting. From pleasing to affirming. Millennials have lived through dial-up internet, the rise of social media, the dawn of smartphones, economic recessions, global pandemics, and the transition from Blockbuster rentals to endless streaming (with zero ads if you pay $6.99 a month). Most millennials may not entirely know how to master the most viral tiktok dances. The fact is, we know how to write in cursive and long division and can read time on clocks with our hands. And this is part of our journey. Part of our blessing.

I recently had the jarring realisation that I have actually reached an age where everything seems to have happened a mere two or three years ago. When actually, they likely happened in 2003. For those who need a minute to do the math, it was over twenty years ago! Without making you feel too aged, I have to state that time is relative. You never quite feel the reality of how long a minute is until you exercise. You also never quite feel the reality of what twenty years feels like until you sit down to consider the evolution of your life.

Time has this uncanny ability to slip through our fingers like sand in an hourglass (so are the days of our lives), yet it leaves imprints, moments we cherish, lessons we learn, and connections that last. And as I reflect on it, I realise the real blessing is not just in the passage of time but in the life we build within it. Every year, every challenge, every reunion and heartache, they all come together to make us who we are.

The older I get, the more I realise that time isn't just about ticking clocks or another birthday cake with an absurd amount of candles. It's about the moments when life feels full, those simple, quiet moments where you look around and just feel grateful. It's the morning coffee when the world is still asleep, the sound of my daughters giggling at something only they find funny, the way the sun filters through the curtains, or even those deep sighs of contentment after a long day. Time is the backdrop for all these things, and learning to appreciate it instead of racing against it is perhaps the greatest gift we can give ourselves.

I used to think life was about the big milestones: graduations, promotions, weddings, and the glamorous parts of our timelines that we felt the need to share. But now, as I inch toward my 40s, I see that the true magic is in the little things, the seemingly insignificant moments that often go unnoticed. Time softens our perspective. The things that once felt like make-or-break moments have faded into lessons learned, while the quieter, unexpected moments have become treasures. Life, with all its ups and downs, is about appreciating both.

Take, for instance, I had a miraculous surprise reunion with one of my most favourite people, Roxanne, on a flight from London to Paris. Twelve years apart, and it felt like we picked up right where we left off. Time didn't erase our bond; if anything, it preserved it, allowing it to make an eighty-minute flight seem like five minutes. We often think time distances us from the past, but sometimes, it brings us full circle to where we're meant to be. That's the beauty of life. The blessing of time is in how it brings us back to the people we love, the lessons we need to learn, and the moments that matter most.

Life is a series of seasons. Some seasons are filled with endless sunshine, while others are a bit more stormy. But time allows us to grow, to weather the storms, and to appreciate the beauty of each season. I've come to see that life is far less about what happens to us and more about how we experience it and how we choose to frame it. The rush of youth often blinds us to the present. We're so busy planning, achieving, and reaching that we forget to be. But now, as I navigate the transition into my 40s, there's this serene understanding that the real gift is in being fully present in the life we've created.

Time has a way of teaching us that it's okay to slow down. It's okay if our to-do lists don't get done in a day. It's okay if our goals shift as we change.

There's a blessing in letting go of the need to rush toward some illusive finish line and simply allowing ourselves to evolve, to grow at our own pace. The beauty of life isn't in how quickly we can accomplish things but in how fully we can live through each experience.

One of my most surreal experiences was at a Boyz II Men concert. Yes, I'm talking about the legendary R&B group we all swooned over in the '90s! There I was, on my 20th Birthday, and due to some mismanagement on the organiser's part, I was escorted to the balcony seats next to the stage. As the 'Men' walked out onto the stage, each holding a long stem red rose and about to break into "Close your eyes, make a wish," Wanya Morris handed me the first rose. My teenage dream had come true. Grinning ear to ear like the goofy fangirl I always was as I tried to keep my cool. It was one of those moments where you blink and think, 'Is this really happening?' And then you realise that, yes, it is happening, and life sometimes gifts you these wild, serendipitous moments. To end off a perfect concert, I then got to meet them, get signed autographs and the real cherry on top : the 'mismanaged organisers' gave me a refund 3 days later. It was an incredible birthday.

While life doesn't always turn out how we planned, it could sometimes turn out even better if we're open to it. Time is full of surprises, and sometimes, those surprises come in the form of standing next to your teenage musical admirer in real life.

So, whilst time feels subjective, especially as a millennial mom. Certain moments in life, like waiting in traffic or getting your kid to bed, may seem endless. While cherished experiences, like vacations or moments of silence, seem to fly by. You blink, and they're gone, leaving you wondering how time sped by so quickly when you were trying so hard to hold onto it. It's almost like time itself is playing a trick on you, speeding up during the good times and slowing to a crawl during the tough ones. You find yourself caught between longing for the seemingly eternal bedtime routine to end and then feeling nostalgic when you realise how fast your child is growing up. Time, in this sense, feels almost like a mischievous tactic - very subjective in how you experience it and frustratingly inconsistent in how it seems to move. Moments of joy and calm disappear in a blink, while the struggles feel eternal.

I often catch myself wishing I could have some time alone. I use a lot of my make-believe wishes on asking for a break, and it mostly happens around the 100th "Mom" of the day. Who can blame me, right? It's almost impossible not to get flustered and even mildly frustrated at the constant need for 'Mom.' Because the truth is, Dad could be sitting right there - but your kid will still need to call for 'Mom'.

Yet, amidst the chaos and the relentless demands, I'm learning to appreciate the fleeting nature of these moments. Time flies by so quickly, and while I sometimes crave solitude, I also recognise that each "Mom" is a reminder of my kid's love and dependence. Those little moments, however exhausting, are blessings I first wished for. They matter more than I realise, as they capture the essence of a stage in life that, while challenging, is filled with irreplaceable memories that I'll cherish long after the calls for "Mom" have reduced per day.

So, here's to the blessing of time, the time we've been given, the time we've lived through, and the time that still lies ahead. It's easy to get caught up in the ticking of the clock, in feeling like there's never enough. But if we can learn to embrace it, to see time not as something slipping away but as something we're living in, it becomes a gift. A gift we're lucky to have.

And that's the thing about life. It may not always be perfect or follow the script we envisioned. Still, if we pay attention, it's filled with unexpected blessings, wonderful surprises, and the beauty of simply being here, in this moment, right now.

Chapter 20

Loyalty.

More Reliable Than Your WiFi - Except When It's Not.

There's something undeniably comforting about knowing who your people are. It's not about numbers or popularity but about depth, the kind of loyalty that runs deeper than convenience. When you've been through the trials of life, you realise how rare and precious it is to have a circle that is loyal to you, not just when things are good but when the tides turn and the sea of life gets rough. And let me tell you, I have been blessed with certain harsh realities that highlight exactly who is loyal and who is blatantly failing in 'playing pretend' mode.

My circle isn't that large, but it's solid. There's an unspoken understanding between us, a quiet assurance that we've got each other's backs. It's not about grand gestures or over-the-top declarations. It's the subtle things, the call when you're struggling, the check-in when you've gone quiet, the laughter that always comes at the perfect time. It's the people who show up without being asked and stay without being needed. They're the ones who don't just applaud your wins but who sit with you during the losses, reminding you that none of this defines your worth.

True loyalty doesn't depend on who's winning, who's losing, or what's in it for them. It's the glue that holds the fabric of real relationships together. And for that, I am grateful every single day.

In a world where people come and go like trends, where loyalty can sometimes feel like a lost art, I've been fortunate enough to build a foundation on it. Whispers or distractions don't sway my circle. They see me, the real me, and love me through the good, the bad, and everything in between. We've created a space where authenticity is celebrated, where vulnerability isn't a weakness but a strength. And that's where loyalty thrives. It lives in the moments when you let down your guard and show who you are, flaws and all, and still find yourself surrounded by love.

It wasn't always like this. I used to think loyalty meant sticking with people no matter what, even if they weren't good for me. I stayed in friendships and relationships far longer than I should have out of some misguided sense of duty. But as I've grown, I've realised loyalty isn't about being loyal to everyone. It's about being loyal to the right people. It's about knowing who deserves that kind of devotion and who doesn't. And once you learn to distinguish between the two, everything changes.

There's power in being selective. There's peace in knowing you don't owe your loyalty to everyone who crosses your path. It's okay to be picky. In fact, it's necessary. Not everyone who smiles on your face is rooting for you behind your back. Some people are there for the season, some for the reason, and then there's the precious few who are there for the long haul.

The truth is that I am blessed. Not because I have everything figured out but because I have a circle that reminds me I don't have to. These are the people who understand that life is messy and that we don't always make the right decisions, but that doesn't define us. They are the ones who remind me that it's okay to be imperfect as long as I'm trying, as long as I'm learning, as long as I'm growing.

So, to anyone who feels like loyalty is a dying virtue, let me assure you it still exists. And when you find it, you hold on tight. It's a rare and beautiful gift to be surrounded by people who love and truly support you, push you to be better, and remind you of your strength when you feel weak.

There's an unspoken expectation that family is supposed to be your safe haven. They're the ones who hold you up when life comes crashing down. That's what I believed, too. But when my dad passed away, that belief was shattered in ways I never imagined. The pain of losing him was unbearable enough, but what followed felt like another kind of death, the slow, heartbreaking realisation that those we considered closest to us had turned against us.

I never thought that in my darkest moment, I'd be outcast by the very people who were supposed to be our support system. But that's exactly what happened when we suddenly lost my Dad. Instead of offering comfort, the people we considered the closest became strangers overnight. There were no warm words, no shared grief, no real empathy. Suddenly, everything became about money. It was as if the moment my father drew his last breath, all sense of family, loyalty, and decency died along with him.

It happened so quickly that we barely had time to process it. One day, we were grieving the loss of our father, and the next, we were defending ourselves from people we had once trusted. They didn't approach us with compassion or understanding; they approached us like vultures circling their prey, ready to tear apart whatever they could salvage for themselves.

The betrayal was so blatant it felt surreal. I remember sitting in rooms where decisions were supposed to be made out of love and logic, and instead, the conversation always shifted to money. Who gets what, who's entitled to this, who deserves that? I couldn't wrap my head around it. Was this what family meant? Was this how quickly people could lose sight of what really matters?

And the worst part? There was no expression of guilt. Not a single sign of remorse. It was like watching people who had turned into someone else entirely, people driven by greed rather than grief. They didn't care about the hole that had just been ripped open in our lives. They didn't care about how we were supposed to pick up the pieces of our shattered world. They cared about themselves, what they could get, and how they could benefit from the loss of someone they loved.

I've always believed that death brings people closer and that it has a way of reminding us what's truly important. But in my case, it tore us apart. It exposed a side of my extended family I never wanted to see. Suddenly, the people who had once been in our corner were on the opposite side, looking at us like we were the enemy. We weren't mourning together; we were at war.

Being hammered by your own flesh and blood leaves a mark. It's a betrayal that cuts deeper than any other because it's unexpected. It feels personal in a way that's hard to explain. How could people we shared holidays with, people we laughed and cried with, people who were supposed to be there for us no matter what, suddenly turn their backs?

It wasn't just about the money, though that was the centre of their focus. It was about loyalty, or the lack of it. It was about trust and how quickly it can be broken. They didn't just betray us with their actions; they betrayed everything we thought our family stood for. The support, the love, the connection all vanished in the blink of an eye.

Looking back, I realise now that loss brings out the truth in people. When everything is stripped away, when the façade drops, you see people for who they really are. And sometimes, the truth is painful. It wasn't just my dad who was gone. The family we thought we had was gone, too. Replaced by people we didn't recognise, people who were more interested in securing their own futures than honouring the man we had all loved.

I've spent countless hours replaying those days in my head, trying to make sense of how we ended up here. Maybe it's easier for them to focus on material things, to distance themselves from the emotional weight of what we are going through. Maybe it's their way of coping, though I'll never understand it. What I do understand is this: their betrayal revealed a truth I needed to see, no matter how much it hurt.

We were outcasted, yes. But in being cast out, we found our own strength. We didn't need the validation of those who had shown us their true colours. We didn't need to fight for their loyalty because it had never been there to begin with. Once we accepted that, we found a different kind of peace, not the peace that comes from external validation, but the peace that comes from knowing who truly stands by you in your time of need.

In the end, betrayal has a way of revealing more than just who people are; it reveals who you are, too. I learned that my family, the real family, isn't defined by blood. It's defined by loyalty, by the people who stand with you when everything is falling apart, by the ones who lift you up instead of tearing you down. We may have lost a lot when my dad died, but we gained clarity. And that clarity, as painful as it was to get, is something I will carry with me for the rest of my life.

I no longer mourn the relationships we lost. They were never what we thought they were. Instead, I focus on the ones who showed up, the ones who remained loyal when it mattered most. At the end of the day, family isn't just about shared blood; it's about shared values, shared love, and the loyalty that holds you together even when the world tries to pull you apart.

There will always come a time when you realise that not everyone in your life is meant to stay. Some are fleeting characters, passing acquaintances who drift in and out like the changing seasons. But then there are the ones who remain, the ones who show up for the highs and the lows, the ones whose loyalty runs deep, not out of obligation but out of genuine love. And when you find those people, you begin to understand what it means to be blessed.

Chapter 21

The Search for Purpose.

Like Looking for Your Glasses Whey They're on Your Head.

So here we are, standing at the crossroads of purpose and legacy. A curious intersection where questioning your existence and PTA emails all collide. I think it's safe to assume that if you are reading this book, you are likely at a stage in your life where you start wondering if there's something bigger to life than picking up after people and figuring out what gluten even is. Finding purpose sounds noble as if it should come with a cape and a soundtrack. But in reality, it's more like, "How many people am I responsible for today, and is it okay if one of them doesn't have appropriate shoes on?"

Somewhere between your 30th and 40th birthday, a little tingle starts to make its debut. It is usually accompanied by a subtle voice that whispers, "am I living my purpose?" You may find that this looming question sneaks up on you when you are likely doing something quite mundane. Like wiping slime or glue off the kitchen counter. Or maybe even whilst sitting in the dentist's chair, trying to take your mind off what's going on in your mouth. More often than not, this voice is usually a little louder right after you've spent too much time scrolling through motivational quotes on your social media feed from profiles likely named Sky Quotes or Motivational Moms 101.

It's not that you didn't have a purpose before, you absolutely did! But let's be honest, back then, your purpose was all about survival: "Keep the kids alive, don't die at work, and for the love of everything holy, remember where you parked the car!" Now, let me take you back to one of my "survival mode" moments; I was pregnant and panicked at one of Oprah's women empowerment talks.

I was four months pregnant and seated in the second row - prime seating, right? Wrong. The screens on the sides of the stage were massive, and I had to crane my neck like a giraffe to see anything on the physical stage. The fact is, that my nausea threshold is exceptionally low on a good day. Now, adding pregnancy and all wonderful feels that goes with that, certainly amplified my general nausea with vertigo. So there I was, front and center, neck like a giraffe. That's when the nausea hit, just as Oprah made her grand entrance. My ship started sinking, fast. I started sweating bullets and felt claustrophobic. It was a full-on "I'm-about-to-pass-out-or-vomit" situation. I couldn't walk out - not with Oprah right there! I wasn't even showing with a decent sized preggy bump, so there'd be no flashing my belly for sympathy as I tried to exit. I could either be the rude woman making a dramatic escape or publicly announce, "I'm pregnant and about to pass out!"

So, I did what any overly polite, nauseated person would do - I half crawled, half walked out of the row, apologising to everyone along the way.

Stepping outside, I gulped down air like I'd just escaped a smoke-filled room, desperately trying to steady my spinning head. Deep breaths. "You're okay, you're okay," I whispered, willing myself to regain some semblance of composure. Once the world stopped tilting, I slinked back into the auditorium, this time hovering by the back wall. The talk continued, and by some small miracle, I managed not to hurl.

And here's the kicker: despite that near meltdown, I got to meet Oprah. There's even a perfectly framed photo of our special moment on my desk - a testament to my triumphant survival, and a daily reminder that sometimes, you just have to breathe, fake a smile, and hope for the best. But the real story began when I tried to leave. For 30 sweaty minutes, I roamed the parking lot, dragging every car guard in sight with me, desperately searching for my white BMW. The sun was relentless, my frustration mounting by the second. Just then, my phone rang - it was my assistant, reminding me I had a meeting in 15 minutes. "Yeah, I know, Stace... but here's the thing - I can't find my car," I replied, as sweat dripped down my face and the guards exchanged worried glances.

Then it hit me - like a ton of bricks. I wasn't even driving my car. Nope, I had taken Roux's. In two seconds flat, I found it and casually slid into the driver's seat, sitting there in stunned silence. The absurdity of it all. The sheer ridiculousness of spending half an hour hunting for the wrong car, hit me like a punchline. And as I sat there, laughing at my own ridiculousness, a strange realisation started to creep in.

How many times in life had I been frantically searching for something, only to realise I'd been looking in the wrong place all along? How often had I been so caught up in the chaos of life, in the survival of it all, that I missed the bigger picture? Probably more often than I'd like to dwell on.

Back to finding your purpose. In your 20's and 30's, your purpose was probably more 'driven' than it feels like it would be heading into your 40's. Now, you're wondering if maybe you're supposed to be someone, not just someone's something.

The issue is (and it's my fault for bringing it up) that purpose sounds like this monumental, unshakable thing, like the north star of your soul. But here's the secret: purpose is often softer than you'd expect. It doesn't necessarily arrive with a parade and confetti. Sometimes, it just shows up in your shopping cart at the supermarket, disguised as some fresh blueberries or bananas or carrots.

And then there's the "legacy" part. At 40, you start thinking, "How will I be remembered? Will my children think I was a goddess of wisdom or just the lady who knew where all the remote controls were hidden?" Legacy can feel like a lot of pressure. Like, what are we supposed to leave behind? A memoir? A charity? A better recipe for banana bread?

Maybe it's time to rethink legacy. It doesn't have to be grand or immortal. You don't need to be the next Oprah or build a space station. Your legacy could be teaching your kids empathy, kindness, and the ability to find joy in a world full of chaos. It could be the way you mentored someone at work or helped a friend through a tough time. Or it could be your secret blueberry jam recipe that will be passed down to future generations.

Perhaps the most ridiculous part of all this legacy talk is that we often imagine it will arrive after we're gone, like it's not something you need to be thinking about now, right? But the truth is, legacy is happening right now!

It's in the laugh lines your friends have because you made them laugh too hard at wine night. It's in the lives you've already touched, sometimes in small, quiet ways that don't make headlines but make heartlines (possibly not a real thing, but it sounds real, and it's part of my legacy to make it a real thing!)

Here's another thing nobody tells you: purpose changes. It's not this static, never-changing thing that you figure out once and then carry around, dispensing parts of it everywhere you go. What lit you up at 25 might feel stale at 40. And that's okay. In fact, it's more than okay, it's necessary.

At 25, maybe your purpose was about climbing the career ladder, achieving success, or proving yourself. But at 40? Maybe your purpose is about finding joy in the in-between moments, savouring the space you've carved out in this messy, chaotic world. Maybe your purpose is less about achieving and more about being present, being thoughtful, and, my favourite part, being unapologetically you.

Perhaps it's not about 'finding a purpose' at all. Perhaps it's about collecting reasons for purpose along the way. Some days, your purpose might be to inspire your kids to build a fort. On other days, it may be to exhibit Monica (Friends reference again) type tidiness and order.
Whichever it is, it's important that we re-evaluate the impact we expect a legacy to stand for. Forget about statues and Nobel Prizes. Your impact is often felt in small but mighty ways. It's in the way you made your friends feel when you listened. It's in the hugs you give, the laughter you share, and the stubborn refusal to give up when life feels like a perpetual Monday.

Rather, consider teaching as part of your legacy, whether it's teaching your kids to make a bed or pack a dishwasher or explaining the meaning of supercalifragilisticexpialidocious. Pass on your wisdom, no matter how big or small. This is all part of your legacy and purpose. Along with your values, the way you bring them to life, and the way you live up to them.

In the end, finding purpose and leaving a legacy doesn't have to be as serious or as overwhelming as it sounds. Your purpose could change daily. Sometimes, it's about making an impact, and sometimes it's just about finding clean socks. Your legacy might be profound, or it might be the fact that you raised good humans or wrote the funniest Facebook statuses.

The truth is: the more you focus on living a life that feels authentic and joyful to you, the more you'll build a legacy that matters. And trust me, people will remember your laughter far longer than your LinkedIn profile. So, whether your legacy has a lasting impact or simply the best carrot cake ever - own it. You're writing it every day, one laugh, one hug, and one ridiculously unglamorous Tuesday afternoon at a time.

Chapter 22

Hello, 40.

Midlife Mantra: I'm Too Old For This Shit.

Welcome to midlife, where last night's wild discussions turn into this morning's thrilling exchange of salmon recipes and vacuum cleaner links. 'Here are those hot links we chatted about, ladies!'

Sound familiar? If yes, then you are well on your way. If not, then brace yourself.

I had always thought of "midlife" as something for other people, perhaps for the women in stretchy pants power-walking through the mall with oversized sunglasses, talking about Pilates and "finding themselves." But then, one day, as I stood at the playground surrounded by other moms, I realised with bone-chilling clarity: Oh my God, I'm one of them.

Saying goodbye to your 30s as a woman feels a bit like bidding farewell to an old frenemy, one you've had a wild, confusing, and occasionally enlightening time with but are more than ready to part ways. Your 30s were like that chaotic decade where you were supposed to "have it all figured out," but truth be told - you didn't. You spent half the time juggling responsibilities, pretending to love kale, and googling "how to be a successful adult" at 2 a.m. Yet, somewhere between the career hustle, relationship puzzles, and metabolism that decided to take early retirement, you survived. Thrived even. But let's be real, those late nights and questionable life choices came with some regrets, mainly the unnecessary stress of trying to please people you don't even like.

So, here's to kiss your 30s goodbye with a dramatic wave and zero tears. Sure, you've gained some life lessons, like realising no one knows what they're doing and that brunch is more about the mimosas than the food. Want to know the best part? You're walking away with fewer hangovers, less FOMO, and a lot more self-respect. As you head into 40, it's no longer about being perfect; it's about being unapologetically yourself. Because let's face it, the only thing you're chasing in your 40s is your dreams. And maybe an earlier bedtime.

• • •

It all started innocently enough, scrolling through Instagram, mindlessly double-tapping pictures of influencers living their best lives. There they were, basking in the glow of perfect sunsets, holding a latte in one hand and some obscure wellness product in the other. It didn't seem that hard, right?

Take a photo, add a filter, slap on a quirky caption, and boom - you're a modern-day icon.

Somewhere between my third cup of coffee and a particularly inspirational quote about chasing your dreams, I made the decision: I was going to make my account public and try my best to market myself as an accomplished Author and, hopefully, with a few things worth saying.

I was fully convinced that my life could be fascinating enough to document for the world. "People need to see this," I thought to myself as I posted a picture of my dog sitting in a cardboard box. I tagged it #BoxLife and waited for the likes to roll in.

They did not.

But I wasn't deterred. After all, every influencer of sorts has to start somewhere, right? Besides, my followers (all 152 of them) just hadn't discovered my brilliance yet. I decided I needed a plan, a strategy. Surely, real influencers have those.

I spent hours diving into the depths of "How to Boost your personal brand on Instagram" blogs, YouTube tutorials, and hashtag generators. I downloaded apps to track my follower count, planned my "content strategy," and even created a posting calendar. Mondays would be #MotivationMonday; I know it is not very original. But here, I think that in order to be relevant, your tags have got to be relevant and, therefore, used extensively. My thought was that I'd share inspirational quotes about how I 'totally' have my life together (cue fake laughs). Wednesdays?

#WhatIEatWednesday, a close-up shot of the quinoa salad I'd probably never eat again. Sundays? Oh, Sundays were for #SelfCareSunday with bubbles in the bath, a glass of wine, and a candle lit in the background for aesthetic purposes.

By the end of the week, I had my first batch of content ready to go. I even drafted captions like:

"Here's to chasing dreams and sipping lattes #Blessed #GrindTime #LatteLife"

I felt ready. This was it, the start of my public profile social media journey.

Post number one: A beautifully filtered shot of my morning coffee, steam curling in the sunlight, a motivational quote typed out in delicate cursive underneath: "Rise and grind, the world is yours to take!" I watched the likes come in, well, two likes, from my mother and an old college friend who probably felt sorry for me.

On day two, I posted a selfie with the perfect lighting. The caption read: "Life is short, make it sweet #NoFilter (but there was totally a filter)." This one raked in five likes. Five! I could practically hear the champagne corks popping in my head.

Then it happened. I got my first comment.

It was from my aunt.

"Awww, sweetie, you look so beautiful! Hope you're doing well. Remember to call your cousin."

And just like that, reality smacked me in the face. Not only was my social persona off to a rocky start but now I had to call Naomi.

Despite the slow start, I wasn't giving up. Social media personas don't quit! I began documenting everything. Breakfast? Posted. My workout (which was really just me walking from the couch to the fridge)? Posted. A "spontaneous" selfie that took 27 tries to get, right? Posted.

I curated my feed like a museum exhibit. I spent hours figuring out what colour palette would represent my "brand." Should I go for soft, pastel tones or bright, bold colours? Maybe I could lean into the minimalist aesthetic and post empty white walls with deep philosophical quotes like, "Sometimes, less is more."

Each post became an event. It was no longer about living life, but about curating it in perfect little boxes for the 'gram. I bought a ring light, convinced my phone camera wasn't cutting it, and even ordered a "lifestyle flat lay" set to make my desk shots look artsy. Was I becoming obsessed? Probably. But that's what dedication looks like, right?

Meanwhile, my followers weren't exactly multiplying. I was stuck at 162, which included my mother, my aunt, and my ex-boss (who was definitely just keeping tabs on me). I even tried using those engagement hacks, like following people, liking 100 posts in a row, and leaving comments like "Nice feed! Follow back?" (They never did.)

Then came the day that broke me. I had spent hours setting up the perfect photo of my dog lying in a sunbeam, a carefully placed book next to her, and my coffee just out of focus in the background. The caption? "Just living my best life, one sunbeam at a time #Goals #Blessed."

After posting, I checked my phone obsessively. One like…two likes…four likes. All family. The crushing realisation hit me: the internet was simply not impressed by my carefully curated life.

I had to face the truth, my life was just…normal. Maybe even a little boring.

But here's the thing, I didn't stop. Sure, I may not have a glamorous social media life filled with exotic trips and PR boxes, but I realised that the people who followed me (even if they were mostly related to me) liked me for me.

So, I stopped worrying about whether my feed looked like an influencer's highlight reel. I started posting what made me laugh, what made my day a little brighter, and yes, sometimes even what made me roll my eyes. My follower count may not have skyrocketed, but I found myself enjoying the process again. And who knows, maybe one day I'll hit the big time. But until then, you'll find me right here, sipping my #RealLife coffee, waiting for my mom's next like. Because the truth is, dear reader, I'm too old for this shit.

• • •

In your 30s, you probably spent too much time seeking perfection. The perfect life, perfect body, perfect relationships. By 40, you realise that perfection is a myth, and life is more about progress and embracing your imperfections. The goal shifts from 'doing it all right' to 'doing what feels right'. As millennials, we were taught the art of people-pleasing, but by the time you reach 40, you learn the true power of saying "no" without guilt. Whether it's declining invitations to events that don't bring you joy or walking away from toxic situations, your 40s become about protecting your peace and prioritising yourself.

It's now that we face the hard reality that time is finite and, therefore, invaluable. It's imperative we start spending our time wisely and on things that truly matter to ourselves. Good riddance to societal standards. It's time to bring on balance and fulfilment. By this point in life, it's fair to say that we have lived enough to understand that our worth isn't dependent on others' opinions or validation.

By now, we've endured enough battles (internal and external) to realise that most of the opinions we used to worry about were never really about us at all. They were reflections of other people's insecurities, their unfulfilled dreams, and their projections. Let's stop living for the audience. We become the directors of our own stories, editors of the narratives we wish to tell, and most importantly, we decide which characters stay in our lives and which ones we can finally let go of.

Remember unless you have walked a mile in my shoes or been through my struggles - then your opinion means shit.

There is a quiet confidence that comes with this stage of life, a subtle assurance that doesn't need to be shouted. It doesn't seek validation because the only validation needed is from within. The pressure to conform to be thinner, quieter, and more acceptable begins to dissolve. In its place is a sense of self that offers a profound understanding that we are enough, just as we are.

Of course, it's not without its challenges. There are moments when the world's expectations can still creep in, but for the woman who is about to reach this milestone, the question is not what the world expects of her, but what she expects from herself. At 40, the rules change. Instead of shrinking to fit, we start expanding into spaces we never thought possible. We rediscover passions, find new ones, and make peace with the fact that life doesn't always follow the script.

The glitches of your 20s? Patched up. The bugs from your 30s? Mostly ironed out. By 40, you're running pretty smoothly - well, except for the occasional chiropractor visit.

Friendships as we head into our 40s are on another level too. Gone are the days of keeping in touch with every person you've ever met, like it's some kind of emotional Survivor game. Chances are, your friends list has whittled down to the essentials: the ride-or-die crew. Those who will show up at your house with wine in hand, when you've had a bad day or those who will laugh with you about the time you accidentally texted your boss about attending a meeting in sweaty Padel gear. And the best part? You're not worried about impressing them. You've seen each other cry, lose your keys for the millionth time, and stumble through life's awkward moments. There's no need for pre-tense. These, are your people.

And when you look at life through this lens, you realise that 40 isn't the beginning of the end, it's the start of something liberating, exciting, and unashamedly you. The journey from people-pleaser to boundary-setting, the no-nonsense goddess, has been hard-earned, but it's the reward of surviving all the small, ridiculous, and sometimes heartbreaking moments that brought you here.

So, what if the world doesn't know how many times you've reinvented yourself? Who cares if Instagram's algorithm never rewards you with more than five likes? You've earned your place in the world, and it doesn't need filters or followers to validate it. At 40, you're living life for yourself, on your terms, with your people, and doing what truly makes you happy. There is a delicious freedom in no longer caring about playing by anyone else's rules. This is life, raw and unfiltered, and it's never been better. So this is a good time to remind ourselves of another great philosopher, Aaliyah, when she said, "Age ain't nothin' but a number." And if that, fellow millennials, is not a reason to give zero fucks, I dont know what is.

In summary, turning 40 is when you realise that life doesn't need to be perfect to be awesome. You've learned to embrace the messy, the imperfect, and the wonderfully weird parts of being human. Life at 40 is about owning who you are, quirks and all, and realising that the best is yet to come because you're finally living on your terms.

Let our 40s be the years we stop chasing approval and start basking in the glow of our own bloody brilliance. Let's step into the next chapter with a heart full of love, a mind full of dreams, and a bottle of champagne on ice because we darn well earned it.

So Dear Reader, as a parting cheers, here is to the next decade, where confidence replaces comparison, happiness beats out perfection, and we finally stop asking permission to be ourselves.

The End.

In Finding 40, Alisha Ramasar invites you on an exhilarating and humorous adventure through the emotional ups and downs of approaching the big four-oh, shedding light on the often-overlooked realities of womanhood. With candid wit, heartfelt honesty, and relatable anecdotes, she delves into the experience of aging, comparing it to savouring a fine wine (or perhaps a long-lost bottle of rosé). Throughout her journey, she emphasises that it's perfectly fine to feel lost and that the chaos of life is what makes it truly exciting. Whether you're already feeling the pressure or still contemplating what lies ahead, Finding 40 serves up valuable insights, sprinkled with humour, for anyone pondering their next chapter.

"This is my way of Finding 40—and if you're ready to dive into this next chapter of life with me, then let's f*cking go for it."
- Alisha Ramasar

wwww.alisharamasar.com
@byalisharamasar